Me, The Jokerman

Also by Khushwant Singh

FICTION

Train to Pakistan
I Shall Not Hear the Nightingale
Delhi: A Novel
The Company of Women
Burial at Sea
The Sunset Club
The Portrait of a Lady: Collected Stories

NON-FICTION

Truth, Love & a Little Malice: An Autobiography
Delhi Through the Seasons
Indira Gandhi Returns
A History of the Sikhs
Ranjit Singh: Maharaja of the Punjab

ANTHOLOGIES

The Freethinker's Prayer Book
99: Unforgettable Fiction, Non-fiction, Poetry & Humour
Portrait of a Serial Killer: Uncollected Writings

TRANSLATIONS

Land of Five Rivers
Umrao Jan Ada (with M. A. Husaini)
Shikwa and Jawab-i-Shikwa
Celebrating the Best of Urdu Poetry (with Kamna Prasad)

Me, The Jokerman

enthusiasms, rants & obsessions by

KHUSHWANT SINGH

edited by Mala Dayal

ALEPH

ALEPH

ALEPH BOOK COMPANY
An independent publishing firm
promoted by ***Rupa Publications India***

First published in India in 2016
by Aleph Book Company
7/16 Ansari Road, Daryaganj
New Delhi 110 002

ISBN: 978-93-84067-51-9

1 3 5 7 9 10 8 6 4 2

For Naina,
who her grandfather hoped would
write more and better stories than him.

CONTENTS

EDITOR'S NOTE

'Khushwant Singh, the writer of joke books?' the shopkeeper in Nainital asked, when we enquired if he had any books by the author. The perception of the Nainital shopkeeper was not only based on the author's popular joke books but also on Khushwant Singh's witty, light-hearted, engaging weekly columns.

This aspect of the man has often overshadowed his considerable contribution as a writer of memorable fiction—*Train to Pakistan*, *I Shall Not Hear the Nightingale* (now renamed *The Lost Victory*), *Delhi: a Novel*—short stories and non-fiction. The seminal two-volume *A History of the Sikhs* is even today essential reading for anyone interested in the Sikhs or Sikh history.

This collection, culled from the articles and columns that he wrote in the magazines and newspapers he edited and contributed to—the *Illustrated Weekly of India*, *New Delhi*, the *Hindustan Times*, *The Tribune*, etc.—reflects his intense concern about growing fundamentalism, curiosity about godmen and women and the state of the country and its people. There are also evocative pieces on nature and amusing vignettes on the cities he lived in—Delhi and Bombay and the hill station he escaped to in the summer, Kasauli. Included is a diary from January to November of the traumatic year 1984. Inevitably, the book concludes with 'Sex Matters' and a selection of jokes.

Mala Dayal,
New Delhi,
July 2016

PERSONAL HISTORY

SENTINEL DOGS

My housekeeper in Kasauli had two dogs to keep uninvited visitors and monkeys at bay—Neelo and Joojoo. Neither could claim any pedigree and had been picked out of the litters of bitches living in the vicinity. Both were ill-tempered but their barks were stronger than their bites. They were never known to bite anyone, but everyone, including the postman, shouted his arrival from a distance. When they had no one to bark at, they growled at each other and often had a scuffle. Their ill temper was more in evidence when I happened to be in Kasauli. As is common to most dogs, they sense who is the master of the house and attach themselves to him rather than those who feed them. No sooner would I arrive, the two would vie with each other to claim closeness to me. Neelo being the younger and tougher of the two would sit by my chair and snarl at Joojoo if he came anywhere near me. But Joojoo found ways to get round his rival. Neelo did not like to go for a stroll in the evening and would wait for me at the gate. I did not like Joojoo coming with me because he was prone to pick quarrels with any dog we met on our walks. I did my best to shoo him back home but he found footpaths on the hillside to catch up with me. While going through the small stretch of the bazaar, Joojoo would fight half a dozen dogs belonging to shopkeepers. However, over the years I got used to the temperaments of the two dogs and stopped fussing about them.

This went on for fourteen years. Both Neelo and Joojoo aged but not very gracefully. White hair sprouted round their mouths, they became slower in their movements, Joojoo stopped dogging my footsteps during my evening strolls. I noticed signs of ageing in the two dogs but refused to admit to myself that I too had aged and was often reluctant to step out of the house.

When I returned to Kasauli in June, Neelo was missing. My servant told me that the dog-men in the employ of the Cantonment Board had fed him poison because he wore no collar. Joojoo, who had spent his lifetime quarrelling with Neelo, looked older than ever before. His skin sagged over his bones, his genitals hung like a dilapidated sack under his belly, his legs trembled as he walked and his eyes looked bleary and unseeing. He would join me at teatime to beg for a biscuit or two because he could not chew anything harder. One morning he came and sat by me while I was having my morning tea. When I got up, he stood up on his trembling legs and looked pleadingly at me. I spoke to him gently: 'Joojoo tu budhdha ho gaya. Joojoo main bhee budhdha ho gaya (Joojoo you have got old, so have I).' He looked at me with uncomprehending eyes and slowly went away. An hour later, one of the boys living in the house came and told me: 'Joojoo mar gaya (Joojoo is dead).' I saw him lying by the club house. The Cantonment Board took his body away in a cart. So ended our fifteen-year-long friendship.

(2002)

'SECULIAR' STATE

Many friends of my university days have made good in the films. There is Balraj Sahni (and his son Parikshit); Chetan Anand and his brother Dev Anand; my own cousin Achala Sachdev; and Kamini Kaushal whose father, Professor Kashyap, was my tutor. There is also Rajbans Krishen Khanna, an associate from the halcyon days of passionate leftism. It is good to see them prosper, to enjoy their lavish hospitality, to bask in the sunshine of their popularity. What a vicarious thrill to be seated alongside a friend and hear a pretty teenager scream with excitement: 'That's Balraj Sahni!' Sometimes I get envious. Why doesn't someone jump with joy and yell, 'There's the editor of the *Illustrated Weekly*!'

Envy is the mother of malice and malice can let loose barbed shafts. This one is aimed at Rajbans Khanna. He has launched a most laudable venture, viz., a film on the epic voyage of the *Komagata Maru*—a Japanese vessel chartered by Sikh emigrants on their way to Canada in 1914. After much violence the ship was turned back, over thirty of its passengers were killed in a fracas at Budge Budge harbour near Calcutta; the remnants became the nucleus of the Ghadr rebellion in the Punjab. Later many turned Communists. It's just the theme for Rajbans who is a Punjabi, a dedicated Marxist and, I presume, an atheist.

Rajbans invited me to a religious ceremony prior to the shooting of the film. The one-foot-long card was very appropriately dyed in revolutionary red. It had an equally appropriate quotation from Iqbal exhorting the poor of the world to rise and destroy the mansions of the rich, burn down the crops of those who do not feed the hungry. The function was to be presided over by the chief minister of the Punjab, Gurnam Singh, an ardent Akali, passionately anti-Communist and almost certainly a non-participant in a Hindu muhurat. However, he had given money for the enterprise. And although he was unable to be present, the ceremony was duly performed with the chanting of mantras and cracking of coconuts. And why not! It is truly said ours is not a secular but a *seculiar* state?

Rajbansji is not alone in this confusion of thought. Samuel Butler has written of a man who, when asked what his religion was, replied, 'I am an atheist, thank God!'

I am reminded of Harold Morland's verse, 'Fair Play', on a lady of similar ambivalence of mind:

A pious self-respecting dame.
With British breadth of mind.
Not only at the sacred name of Jesus Christ her head inclined.
But she behaved the very same when Satan's mentioned.
'Really!' said the priest, 'your courtesy is odd to say the least.
For after all, the Devil isn't God!'

But the lady's ready with her counter-blow:

'You of all men, Vicar, understand—civility costs nothing, and you never know!'

(1969)

THE POISON PEN

I am on the horns of a dilemma. I have been sent a book to review. Its contents are false, its intent malicious, its potential for mischief infinite. I have always protested against every kind of censorship. But this book makes me reconsider my thoughts on the subject because it represents to me the ultimate in obscenity. I would gladly make a bonfire of it in every marketplace. What am I to do? If I vent my spleen by saying nasty things about it I give it undeserved publicity—and perhaps *boost* its sales amongst people whose minds are as perverse as that of the author. I could make fun of it, I could ignore it. Earlier when I tried both with some books of the same genre I found to my dismay that the derision missed its mark—and my advice to readers to treat such works with contemptuous disdain also had no effect. The books pretend to be works of historical research. They claim to prove that monuments like the Qutab Minar and the Taj Mahal were not of Muslim but Hindu origin. Despite being patently absurd I now find that many people are taking them seriously. Their authors are invited to address university audiences. I have reason to believe that what they say is eagerly lapped up by college greenhorns. The books are sold outside the monuments. Professional guides utter their spurious contents to gullible parties of visitors. One can explain why counterfeit currency will go on circulating. Distort your facts, inject a dollop of pride in your own race and religion, prejudice and contempt for that of others and you have a witches' brew of hate which can be easily brought to boil.

Let me give you a few examples from this book. Like earlier publications of its kind, it seeks to prove that a complex of seventeenth -century Muslim edifices was in fact built earlier by Hindus. The walls are inscribed with references to their origin. These the author dismisses as graffiti '...the very nature of the Muslim inscriptions reveals that they are all frivolous scribblings of idle hands, such as one sees at picnic spots, idle revellers or pleasure-seekers are known to scrawl irrelevant and incoherent abracadabras at impossible places at the historic or safe places they visit. Muslim inscriptions on Indian buildings [the author really means Hindu] are exactly of that type.' The word 'frivolous' appears to be the author's takiya kalam—pillow word. Hence, he concludes that like every other inscription here the one crediting Akbar as the builder of the monument in question 'too is frivolous—the idle work of an idle man with an idle fancy who wanted to make idle money from Akbar by engraving just anything anywhere'.

The walled city of palaces has a complicated network of water channels and hammam baths. This is taken as irrefutable proof of its pre-Muslim origin. 'Muslims take a bath only once a week if at all,' the author assures us. 'They have a desert tradition. They have no use for running water.'

And in any case the earlier invaders were 'mostly illiterate barbarians'. Their only contribution to this building was to 'clog the intricate Hindu water supply system by misusing the tanks for dumping filth and Hindu images'. The author then makes a blanket judgement. 'Raising statues is a sacred Hindu custom, demolishing them is a Muslim penchant.' And so on.

If you were the reviewer, how would you deal with such literature? Abuse and difference are of no avail. Will an appeal to the patriotic sentiment yield better results? Let me try. I base my appeal on the following grounds. One: our history is that of a people divided by race and religion with each section trying to dominate the other by violence and vandalism. No group can point an accusing finger at the other. If the Muslims killed and destroyed, the non-Muslims (e.g. Rajputs, Jats, Marathas and Sikhs) did no less. Two: Our history is not a simple annal of Hindu-Muslim confrontation. In most (if not all) conflicts, there were Hindus on the side of Muslims and Muslims on the side of Hindus. It is a proven fact of history that in India more Muslim blood was shed by Muslims than by Hindus. Three: through all the centuries of association runs a strand of mutual respect and affection which made it possible for us to create a common culture. Thus, for example, monuments like the Qutab, the Taj and Fatehpur Sikri, though essentially Saracenic in concept (you can see the similarity in hundreds of mosques and mausolea in West Asia), were often executed by Hindu artists and craftsmen and therefore became Hindu-Muslim art, which we can rightly describe as Indian. Four: it is both historically wrong and morally unfair to cater to chauvinistic pride and prejudice. If you brainwash the younger generation with this venomous mixture of distorted fact, fancy and specious argument, you will forever be the real authors of communal discord. You will be the real perpetrators of what has happened in recent weeks in many cities and towns of Gujarat—the murder of the spirit of Gandhi. If we fail to make ourselves into one nation, you will be the authors of that failure.

You no doubt want to know the name of the book and its author. I won't tell you. If I can help it, not one naya paise will go to the author or his publisher.

(1969)

1984: A DARK YEAR

JANUARY

For many years I ushered in the New Year drinking champagne and embracing women I scarcely knew. Most of the following morning was spent nursing a hangover and resolving never to touch liquor again. After middle age overtook me I made no distinction between New Year's Eve and other nights. While others were drinking, dancing, singing and popping balloons, I would go off to sleep and the New Year would steal over me as I snored. I would rise at 4.30 a.m., switch on the BBC and listen to the news. This year was no different. The telephone rang. It was a call from Bombay, a voice from the distant past I could barely recognize wished me a happy New Year. It was like 'breeding lilacs out of the dead land, mixing / Memory and desire, stirring / Dull roots with spring rain'.

Daylight broke through the mist. It was cold. The tops of the trees caught the orange of the morning sun and the dew-drenched lawn sparked in the sunlight. A woodpecker lighted on the siris tree and crackled 'noo-noo-year, noo-noo-year'.

At breakfast, the widow of a cousin who had died on New Year's Eve the previous year came to reminisce about her husband. On the birth of a new year we talked of death. In the afternoon Shahidul Haq and Himayatuddin of Bangladesh dropped in. Himayat's wife was expecting their second child. 'We hoped she (they already have a son) would be born on New Year's Day,' said Himayat's wife. For a change on the birth of the New Year we talked of a new life to come. The next visitor was my latest heart-throb, a lovely girl saddened by her experience of life. She unburdened her heart which she has never given to anyone yet. But a fellow who pursued her with flattery, gifts and proposals of marriage turned out to be a philanderer. She was relieved she discovered the truth about him in the nick of time, but she was sad that the year should begin with betrayal.

I acquired my new Maruti. It is a lovely little car which taxi drivers contemptuously describe as sabun-daani, a soap dish. I took K. K. Birla for a joyride and told him it was half the price and twice as good as the Birla product, the Ambassador.

The following week I ran into Jacqueline Kennedy and her son John. We had an hour together in the VIP lounge at Palam. She looked her years and was somewhat incoherent in her speech. I could not believe a woman like her could have sold herself to an obnoxious character like Aristotle Onassis for his billions; nor that her handsome son could, after the assassinations of his father and uncle, want to become a politician. I had John over for dinner and asked him who he would like to meet, politicians or pretty girls? Without hesitation he replied, 'Politicians.' However, I asked both. He ignored the girls and spoke only to politicians.

This was followed by an evening with Namita and Rajiv Gokhale. Her novel *Paro* will be published in London. She was bubbling with excitement. Then presided over a poetry reading by the policeman-poet, Keki Daruwalla. Two lines struck me as prophetic:

> During the big drought which is surely going to come
> the doves will look up for clouds, and it will rain hawks.

It continued to be very cold. But the chill winds did not dampen the enthusiasm of our birds, woodpeckers still cluster about the siris. Every morning painted storks wheel in the blue skies, flying and heading for the Jumna.

How is it I overlooked the most important day in January? The Gantantra Diwas on the 26th? Because over the years my enthusiasm for celebrating anything has been diminishing. Shame on me.

FEBRUARY

Despite the severe cold, the cherry tree has blossomed. If the cherry flowers are here can spring be far behind? Asha and Vasanth Seth (Great Eastern Shipping) dropped in. He says Bombay has become so congested that the only way he can get fresh air is by sleeping in his yacht anchored offshore. His holidays are spent sailing among the creeks. If every Bombayman owned a yacht, we could walk over the sea to Karachi.

I have two birthdays—one official and the other nearer the real date of nativity. I do not celebrate either of them. But there are friends who never fail me on 2 February. Inder Malhotra of the *Times of India* is a born birthday greeter. So are the Advanis who lived in the apartment above mine in Colaba. Jyoti never forgets to send me a telegram. This year there was nothing much to celebrate. Bhindranwale was causing me acute anguish. I wrote a profile of the 'Sant' for Hyderabad's *Newstime* describing him as a 'mad monk'. One of these days his goons will get me. Little did he know that he would not be around on my next fake birthday.

A heavy mist spread over the city on the morning of the 4th and brought air services to a standstill. My flight to Islamabad to attend a journalists' meet organized by *The Muslim* was delayed by two hours; I missed the connecting flight at Lahore and had to spend the night and next day in the city which had been my home till Partition and where many of my dearest friends are buried. I rang them up (the living) and next morning had a lobby full of my Pakistani brothers, their wives and children. They were worried over India's aggressive postures. The latest case was the disappearance of two servants of an Indian diplomat from Islamabad. Our embassy protested against their abduction. The protest boomeranged as a few days later both men surfaced in India (nobody knows how they got across the border).

Three days in Pakistan listening to speeches from their foreign minister, I & B minister and retired generals protesting their goodwill towards India was assuring. More than India they were worried by the Russian presence in Afghanistan.

I returned home to a Punjab coming to the boil. The Punjab bandh was total. It was followed by Hindu-Sikh riots in Punjab and a massive Hindu backlash in Karnal, Panipat and Yamunanagar, resulting in considerable loss of Sikh lives and property. At the Golden Temple there was an exchange of fire between Bhindranwale's men and the armed police. When will Akali leaders and Bhindranwale's gunmen realize that for what they do in the Punjab the price is paid by Sikhs living in other parts of India? In India life is cheap. What are half a dozen men stabbed to death when a few rail bogeys off the track can take a toll of over forty lives as one did near Ballabhgarh?

I spent three days with President Zail Singh. I flew with him in his plane to Poona. He proceeded by helicopter to Rajkot to garland the statue of Shivaji. On board were his daughter and her husband, also the grandson who had earned his displeasure for shooting pigeons in Rashtrapati Bhavan. None of the family could have known that the angel of death hovered over some members of his family.

I rejoined him in Bombay. All next morning I was on his yacht while he took the salute from ships and submarines of the Indian navy lined off the sea from the Gateway of India. The naval review was a boring affair—ship after ship with its crew lined on the deck, doffing their caps and yelling 'Rashtrapati Ji ki Jai'. I caught glimpses of Indira Gandhi, Rajiv and Sonia who were on the yacht following ours. Throughout the two hours that the ordeal lasted I could see Indira Gandhi going up and down the deck, tireless as ever.

When I got back home to Delhi it had turned cold again. The sky was overcast and it started to drizzle. However, the weather did not dampen the spirits of parliamentarians who reassembled on the 23rd. Affairs of Punjab should have been given top priority; the President scarcely mentioned them in his address to the two Houses.

Salman Rushdie came to India on the invitation of *Gentleman* magazine. After addressing a select audience at the India International Centre, he and Anita Desai, who was among the last six novelists under consideration for the Booker Prize, dropped in for a drink. The next evening (27th) Salman addressed a large gathering on politics and the novel—he blew to smithereens pretensions of the Raj novelists like Paul Scott, Kayo, and even E. M. Forster for not really knowing India or Indians.

MARCH

At a lunch given by Murli Deora at the Taj in Bombay I was told of Prabha Dutt's death in Delhi. I slipped out of the party to return to my room to shed tears of tribute to my grey-eyed young colleague whom I had admired, respected and loved. It was a sad homecoming—first to call on Prabha's husband, 'Speedy' Dutt, and a few days later to hear of the passing of another friend, I. S. Johar (11th), in Bombay and writing to his re-united ex-wife Rama Bans.

March is in some ways one of our two 'autumns'. Neem, peepul and mahua shed their leaves to don new ones for the summer. The days began to lengthen and spring slowly turns to summer with the koel's full throated cry and the barbets incessant calling to each other.

March is named after Mars, the god of war. Very appropriately the Soviets promised massive military aid to help us preserve our freedom against foreign intervention. Meanwhile we had plenty of violence within the country. There were fisticuffs in the Bengal Assembly (19th); a third attempt was made on the life of Darbara Singh, chief minister of Punjab (17th) and on the 19th H. S. Manchanda was murdered in broad daylight by Sikh terrorists. It was ironic as Manchanda was the only Sikh member of a Hindu family.

The Rajya Sabha shed a third of its members to make way for a new batch. This time most of them were picked by Rajiv Gandhi—hence Suresh Kalmadi's pejorative for the Upper House as 'Rajiv Sabha'. But there were a few notable entrants: the industrialist K. K. Birla (Independent), the newspaperman Desh Bandhu Gupta (Congress I) and the breathtakingly lovely film star Jayalalithaa (AIADMK).

Some literary asides deserve mention. Amongst my visitors was Kenneth Rose, biographer of King George V and Lord Curzon—he came to track down the family of the Munshi of Agra who taught Urdu to Queen Victoria. Gillian Tindall, author of a book on Bombay, gave a talk on places of literature. I played the role of an 'extra' in a film on Amrita Pritam. Historian Dr Ganda Singh and editor Sadhu Singh Hamdard were amongst those awarded the Padma Bhushan. The social worker Bhagat Puran Singh, the 'bearded Mother Teresa of Punjab', got a Padma Shri. All three men were to return these honours three months later.

Not very surprising that the Holi festival (17th) was a dull affair. It was too chilly to dowse people with coloured water and there was not the usual goodwill between the communities to take liberties with each other.

APRIL

It was indeed a cruel month. The hatred simmering in Punjab exploded into violence. Amongst those who were killed were Harbans Lal Khanna, BJP member of Punjab Assembly, and Dr V. N. Tiwari (MP) who had replaced Nargis Dutt in the seat next to mine in the Rajya Sabha. Also a number of Nirankaris including women and children. The terrorists did not spare each other.

To prove that the government's stern measures after taking over the administration had not affected them, the terrorists set fire to thirty-seven railway stations at about the same time of the night (15th).

I made my little contribution to the debate on Punjab and was perhaps the only one to condemn Bhindranwale and the Akalis, and warn the government of the perils of dilatory politics in dealing with incendiary material. The home minister P. C. Sethi scarcely listened to what I or anyone else had to say.

Voices from the past came in the shape of ex-ambassador Ellsworth Bunker and his wife, Carol Laise. He is in his nineties; she almost thirty years younger. Both have innumerable Indian friends and visit India every year. This was Ellsworth's last visit to Delhi; he died a few months later.

By mid-April we were in mid-summer. The siris which had perfumed the breezes of spring shed its pompoms; neem flowers were strewn on tarmac roads like layers of sawdust. Agitated lapwings tossed about by hot, squally winds were deliriously demanding 'did-ye did-ye do it? did-ye-do it?' The elite have been swarming to bathing pools; in the evenings anti-mosquito squads pump anti-mosquito smoke over the city; at night the hum of mosquitoes is louder than the roar of traffic.

The winter that we experienced this year was colder than past winters; the summer warmer than most summers, with temperatures soaring into the mid-forties and staying there for many days and nights. Even the seasonal dust storms followed by hail did not cool the hellfires. This year there were not as many electricity breakdowns but many taps ran dry when the need to slake thirst and wash sweat away were the acutest.

Vir Sanghvi and Malavika Rajbans came to interview me for *Imprint*. Their piece would be the instrument of my final breach with Maneka Gandhi and her mother.

Summer brings many aches and pains. One evening of indiscreet drinking gave me gout. At Bharat Ram's party on the birth anniversary of his father, Sir Shri Ram (founder of the DCM empire), I ran into a childhood friend, Lala Pratap Singh. Because of arthritis of the knee he could barely walk. On the other hand his wife, Savitri (daughter of Shri Ram's brother Sir Shankar Lal), had overcome cancer which had only a couple of years ago been declared incurable.

Events in Punjab were fast moving towards a denouement. My friend, Ramesh Chandra, son of Lala Jagat Narain, was gunned down. Hindu-Sikh riots followed taking a toll of twenty-eight lives in one day. Not to be outdone, in Maharashtra, organized and well-prepared Hindu mobs carried death and destruction, killing upwards of three hundred poor, defenceless Muslim weavers of Bhiwandi. The jayanti of Gautama the Buddha fell on the 15th, and went by with the usual homilies about his message of tolerance amongst humans.

Sikhs are slowly but surely losing their status as the pampered elite of India. An instance of the growing animus against the community was an article published in the *Sunday Observer* (29 April) which was the subject of a 'Special Mention' in the Rajya Sabha. It was written by one Vatsayana on the Rashtrapati's visit to the Asiatic Society in Calcutta. It made fun of him dyeing his beard with shoe polish, his ignorance of Darwin, the Earth being round and his proclivity for female flesh. This was editor Vinod Mehta's idea of humour. The leader of the House took note of it and when the matter came up before the Press Council the editor was reprimanded.

Mrs Gandhi's quarrel with her daughter-in-law Maneka was extended to include custody of Sanjay and Maneka's child, Feroze Varun Gandhi. Mrs Sunanda Bhandare, wife of Congress MP Murli Bhandare, served notice on Maneka, questioning the way the child was being exploited by her for political purposes. Maneka countered it with similar charges against Mrs Gandhi. Mrs Bhandare was later elevated to the bench of the Delhi High Court.

India was becoming too hot for me. I took off to Libya where I spent a liquor-free week listening to praises of Colonel Gaddafi's *Green Book*. Mrs Gandhi had been in Tripoli a couple of weeks earlier and had received a great welcome. The city was still plastered with her pictures. A few days after her visit an attempt was made on Colonel

Gaddafi's life and reportedly over three hundred Libyans were killed in the shootout. Libya is an uneasy country trying to bridge a gap of centuries within a few years.

JUNE

June 1984 will go down as the most fateful month in the history of independent India. The Indian Army moved most of its units into the Punjab. On the 3rd in an exchange of fire at the Golden Temple eleven people were killed. Akali leaders, as reckless as ever, decided to impede movements of grain outside the state. The final die was cast. The army surrounded Amritsar and cut it off from the country when thousands of pilgrims were there to celebrate the martyrdom anniversary of the founder of the temple, Guru Arjan. A sporadic exchange of fire began between army units and Bhindranwale's men entrenched in the Akal Takht, the parikrama, and three towers that overlooked the temple complex. Curfew was imposed on the city, journalists expelled and strict censorship imposed on news. Whatever we know of the events that followed are what the government decided we ought to know or from unverified versions of those who were witnesses to the ghastly tragedy that followed. However, all are agreed that although the army gave many opportunities to the pilgrims to get out, not many heeded the warning—either because of the erratic imposition of curfew or indecisiveness. After knocking off the snipers atop the towers on the 5th the army stormed into the temple to be met with withering fire from Bhindranwale's men. Tanks were brought in. They smashed their way into the parikrama and blasted the Akal Takht, killing Bhindranwale and most of his closest associates including General (retd) Shabeg Singh and Amrik Singh. Sporadic firing continued for another three days. How many people died? According to the government's White Paper, 92 army personnel and about 543 civilians. The Akali version put the figure of civilian casualties at over five thousand, a large proportion being pilgrims including women and children. Rajiv Gandhi later admitted that over seven hundred army personnel had died in 'Operation Blue Star'. The action created widespread resentment among the Sikhs. Over two thousand soldiers defected from their centres; some were shot, others arrested. Two Sikh MPs, several MLAs and civil servants resigned; many surrendered honours conferred on them.

On 8 June, President Zail Singh and on 23 June, Mrs Gandhi visited the temple and saw the damage done with their own eyes.

For weeks following 'Operation Blue Star' the army combed Sikh temples and villages in pursuit of extremists. To this day no one knows the extent of the loss of life and property entailed by this exercise.

On 10 June we had our first pre-monsoon shower; this was a day before I saw the monsoon bird (*Clamator jacobinus*). On the afternoon of 14 June Maneka stormed into my study, flung a copy of *Imprint* at my face and stormed out of the house. This was followed a week later by a two-page typed letter from her mother, Amtesh Anand; it was delivered by a lawyer who made me sign a receipt. I read only the first para and then put it away among my books. I expected some reaction but not as exaggerated as the one I got. They were not my kind of people—they are self-centred and unconcerned with what happens to other people. I was relieved the association was at an end.

There was a heavy downpour on the 19th followed by rainless days and the return of dust storms. What a month.

JULY

Having done with Punjab, the government turned to neighbouring Kashmir. On the night when all Muslims, including Chief Minister Dr Farooq Abdullah, were celebrating Id, his brother-in-law, G. M. Shah, manipulated the defection of a sizeable number of Dr Abdullah's followers and presented them before an amenable governor, Jagmohan. Farooq Abdullah's ministry was promptly dismissed and replaced by Shah and his turncoats. This was Mrs Gandhi's eidee (Id gift) to Farooq, one-time family friend. Violence erupted in the Valley.

Meanwhile, Sikh terrorists continued to demonstrate that they had not been overcome. On the 3rd they hijacked an Air India plane with 240 passengers abroad and took it to Pakistan. The Pakistan government returned the plane with its crew and passengers but detained the hijackers.

The monsoon continued to be erratic. It rained on the 13th and 14th. I took myself to Amritsar to see the damage done and interview people who had witnessed 'Operation Blue Star'. The city bristled with soldiers, the citizens were resentful, sullen and scared. Contrary to the government's contention that no damage had been done to the Harmandir Sahib, I counted scores of fresh bullet marks on its walls. And, contrary to claims of having preserved the sanctity of the shrine, I saw a notice alongside the Akal Takht saying 'No smoking or drinking allowed here'.

The army had overlooked taking it off when it allowed pilgrims to re-enter. I cited this evidence in my speech on the White Paper in Rajya Sabha (25th) and was jeered by the treasury benches.

Rain or no rain, on the 28th there were more monsoon birds to be seen in gardens and parks than before.

AUGUST

Warm, sultry, drizzly. Punjab was not the only troubled state. Tamil resentment against the treatment meted out to their kinsmen by the Sri Lankan government found expression in the exploding of a bomb (the third such explosion) at Madras International Airport killing thirty-two people. I saw some of the debris when I went to the city at the invitation of the RSS. It seems the only Hindus willing to take a sympathetic view of the plight of the Sikhs and eager to reclaim them as brethren belong to right-wing political and social groups. Meanwhile, government stooges continued their activities in Punjab. To counteract the high priests' verdict of 'guilty' pronounced against Santa Singh Nihang, who flouted Sikh sentiment by undertaking to rebuild the Akal Takht, and Minister Buta Singh who put him up to it, the two organized a Sarbat Khalsa meet in Amritsar to revoke the hukumnamah issued against them. It was an entirely Congress (I) sponsored show. The Akali response to it was to call a world Sikh meet which, though declared illegal, was a much bigger affair.

The government continued its aggressive postures. After ridding itself of a recalcitrant chief minister in Sikkim, subverting Farooq Abdullah's government in Kashmir, it suborned the loyalties of N. T. Rama Rao's followers in Andhra Pradesh. Governor Ram Lal, earlier removed as chief minister of Himachal Pradesh on charges of corruption in his family, dismissed Rama Rao's government and installed turncoat Bhaskar Rao in his place. Rama Rao, who had just got back from the

US after heart surgery, mustered his followers and demonstrated before President Zail Singh in Delhi that he still commanded a majority in the AP Assembly. The opposition parties rallied around N. T. Rama Rao in a massive demonstration of support. Ram Lal was compelled to resign, but Bhaskar Rao was given time to win over more MLAs. Prices ranged from between five to twenty lakhs per defecting MLA.

On the 22nd, Venkataraman was elected vice president. On the 24th, the Rajya Sabha bid farewell to Hidayatullah. The next day Punjab was again in the news with yet another IAF plane hijacked by Sikh extremists to Lahore. Once more Pakistan returned the plane and passengers—this time the hijackers as well.

The monsoon which had been eccentric made up for its sluggishness with four days of heavy showers at the end of the month.

SEPTEMBER

The month started off with heavy rain; better late than never. And the Opposition maintained heavy pressure on the Congress (I) to test its strength in the AP Assembly. Bhaskar Rao's crude attempts to buy support came to naught and on the 15th N. T. Rama Rao was re-crowned chief minister of Andhra Pradesh amidst scenes of jubilation. The Congress (I)'s clumsier attempts to foment communal trouble and use it as an excuse to impose President's Rule resulted in extensive damage to Muslim property and life in Hyderabad.

Punjab affairs seemed to be on the boil. On the 27th, I was in Chandigarh and met Governor Satarawala. I impressed on him the need for more industry in the state to absorb educated young men who would otherwise turn to violence. He made a note of what I said. Three days later the keys of the treasury (toshakhana) were handed over to the head priests and after four months of occupation the army was withdrawn from the Golden Temple complex. Unfortunately, this was done under threat of a massive morcha of Sikhs to liberate the temple; hence the gesture lost the element of magnanimity and touch of healing.

OCTOBER

It is a bad month for assassinations. Not many Octobers ago North

Koreans succeeded in killing seventeen South Koreans including four cabinet ministers in Rangoon. Earlier this month the IRA exploded a bomb in a Brighton hotel which narrowly missed killing Margaret Thatcher, prime minister of England. Our own prime minister was not so lucky. Her two Sikh assassins took no chances, shooting her at close range and pumping over a dozen bullets into her frail body. As if it was not bad enough for men of honour bound to protect her betraying the trust reposed in them, there were Sikhs in the US, England and even in India who were foolish enough to celebrate the murder and invited, within minutes of her death being confirmed, the wrath of the majority community on the heads of the entire community. This bloodbath washed out the goodwill created by the participation of a sizeable number of Hindus in the kar seva of the Harmandir.

NOVEMBER

Anti-Sikh riots broke out in many parts of India, taking a heavy toll of Sikh life and property. Although government spokesmen put the figure of the Sikh dead at a little over a thousand, non-official estimates put it at over six thousand, half of it in Delhi. Equally savage was violence in Kanpur, Calcutta and Bihar. Hundreds of gurdwaras and thousands of Sikh homes, taxis and trucks were burnt. The pattern of violence indicated organized, well-planned action. In most places the mobs were led by members of the Congress party. Hindus, where they could, helped their Sikh neighbours against arsonists and looters who largely came from surrounding villages and jhuggi-jhonpri colonies. Hindu right-wing groups, notably the RSS and BJP, rendered service to their afflicted Sikh brethren. Over fifty thousand Sikhs were rendered homeless.

The administration finally woke up to its responsibility after the orgy of killing, arson and loot had gone unchecked by the police for three days and nights. The lieutenant governor of Delhi was sacked (but oddly enough replaced by the home secretary who should have owned some of the responsibility for earlier inactivity); the police commissioner and many of the PM's security personnel were suspended or transferred. The home minister is yet to explain his own paralysis in the face of crisis.

The one man who rose to supreme heights in the crisis was Rajiv Gandhi. He made a most dignified statement on his mother's assassination and as soon as her body had been cremated (over a hundred heads of states were present at her funeral) he spent the entire night visiting affected areas and ordering the army to put down violence with an iron hand. If he had only done this two days earlier, the story of the Sikhs would have been different.

[*This piece is an edited version of Khushwant Singh's unpublished journal of 1984. There are no entries for May and December—Ed.*]

(1984)

AFTER-DINNER SLEEP

Last month I was in Chandigarh to deliver the first of the Diwan Chand Sharma Memorial Lectures. If they had consulted the late professor through a planchette or a medium he would have said, 'Not that chap! He does a lot of buk-buk on things he knows little about. He is bogus.' However, there I was. I enjoyed myself lashing out at the establishment and respectability as only one who has no one to answer to can do. The best part of the visit was meeting people I had known twenty-five years ago in Lahore. Some I had believed dead were in vigorous health. Others I had considered mediocre were at the top of their professions. Most of them had done better than I. My illusion that I had fought back the years better than they was also shattered.

I take malicious pleasure in the ageing of others but my own ageing I do not notice. I can tell any shrimati who has dyed her hair. When anyone remarks, 'My God! You've gone fat and grey!' I seek reassurance in my dressing room:

> Mirror, mirror, hanging on the wall
> Who is the greyest, the fattest of us all?
> The mirror smiles and replies:
> Since it is with your eye that I spy
> I see the grey tinged with black dye.
> Fat you are; fat you've always been
> Better consult a weighing machine.

I tuck the wisps of grey hair under my turban, pull in my paunch and rejoin my ageing friends. One has a pinched look and moves his jaws like an old woman munching gruel without her dentures. His wife has had a cataract operation; the thick lenses she wears make her eyes bulge like a cow's. Another chap once so proud of his brisk pace through Lawrence Gardens (now Bagh-i-Jinnah) has become like the proverbial sack of potatoes and now walks with his legs wide apart to accommodate his hydrocele. I have to sit on his left side as he is hard of hearing on the right. Another complains of gas trouble. To emphasize the point he raises a thigh. Before he can break wind, I leap out of range and seek sanctuary beside a flame of former times. She rues the paucity of admirers. Very gallantly I express eternal passion. She dismisses me. 'Arrey! Janey bhee dey!' The man on her other side asks me if I have sex problems that affect the aged. I try to laugh him off: 'Who doesn't? When I could I didn't have the courage. And now I have the courage, I don't seem to have the compulsion.' He wags his head sadly. 'Take my advice. You need a daily intake of crushed pearls mixed with arrack of roses.' I don't need his prescription. I need young female company. There is plenty of that on the Punjab University campus. But when I accost a pretty teenager, she gives me a damper: 'Uncle, you've put on a lot of weight, haven't you?'

I belong neither to the young nor to the old. Thou hast not youth nor age. But as it were an after-dinner sleep, dreaming of both.

(1971)

THE MORNING AFTER

Some people begin their mornings with prayer, others with a cup of tea and yet others with the newspaper. I begin my day by surveying how my neighbours are doing after the night before. Most of them are still asleep long after the sun is up. We are late nighters, late risers. We live cheek by jowl. We can see who drinks and what. We shake hands across our balconies, talk to friends on the other side of the road, listen to each other's Vividh Bharati, partake in husband-wife squabbles and bless romances that blossom here at all hours in all seasons.

It's a nice locality with lots of interesting goings-on. The prudes have given it a bad name. Down with the prudes! As I said, we are owls, not larks. The peace of our morning is broken by the chanting of a beggar. He trudges along in the middle of the empty street, vigorously tapping his white cane. Although he is blind he can sense that we are an Indo-Anglian, Sindho-Goan, Bohra-Memon community. He tailors his lines to fit our polyglot ears.

Blindwallah! Blindwallah!
Dey, dey in the name of Allah!
Memsahib, good marneeng
Rabb-il alameen

Sleepers on the pavement shuffle uneasily. A few faces appear in the windows and balconies. Some yawns, some good morning smiles, never a paisa for the blind beggar who starts us on our day.

At 9 a.m. I emerge from my apartment. Three urchins, who live on the pavement outside, are asleep with the sun on their faces and the buzzing of flies in their open mouths. I step over their corpses and proceed on my way. I have to run many a gauntlet—garbage emptied from balconies, betel spit, phlegm, banana skins and lots of children on their way to school. At the temple round the corner, dozens of lepers line the pavement, holding metal cups with their stubby fingers. Two overfed cows are fed by a bald old man who has a beatific smile on his face. Many passers-by touch the cows and pass their sanctified hands across their chests. The overfed cows drop blobs of dung on the pavement. Shopkeepers mumble prayers as they open their stores. Lottery ticket sellers scream, 'Lashday! Lashday!' Hawkers lay out their wares. Transistors begin to blare. It's Vividh Bharati all the way. Snatches of song are handed like batons in a relay race.

It is on my return from the office in the evening that my neighbourhood comes into its own. As soon as my cab pulls up, urchins run up to welcome me. They are the same boys who sleep on the pavement through the morning. 'Nice goods!' offers one. The other recognizes me. 'Arrey, he lives here.' The short welcome is over. They wait in ambush for other cabs which bring pleasure-seekers to our locality after lamplight. I sit on my balcony and watch the lively throng below. A hansom cab pulls up on the other side of the road. A man emerges from the dark and takes orders. Bottles wrapped in brown paper are handed around. While the hansom cab passengers slake their thirst, they chat with the urchins and scan the windows above them.

Lots of pretty girls smile down at them. They smile at the chosen ones, pay off the hansom cab driver and go up. A policeman sauntering along stops to exchange a friendly word with the bottle supplier. The bottle supplier points to the sky to indicate God is good, business is not bad and slips something in the policeman's palm. In my locality we have achieved a very symbiotic relationship between lawbreakers and guardians of the law.

So it goes on till the early hours of the morning. While the city sleeps we keep the vigil. When the city rouses itself, we let slumber overtake us. Everyone who has eyes in his head can see this. Someone should tell the Blindwallah to come by at night. He'd do better business. And in any case a *good eveneen* rhymes better with *rabb-il alameen* than *good marneeng.*

(1971)

RAT RACE

Weird things happen in this city of Bombay! One morning, I am on my way to the office. Other people are on their way to their offices. Hawkers unpacking their wares. Beggars dusting their square yards of pavement; long, orderly queues at bus stops. God in his Heaven and all's right with the metropolis. Suddenly a swirl of crows appears like a black dust devil over Flora Fountain—cawing furiously, dive-bombing in turn over some mobile object on the tarmac. A massive rat comes scampering along the pavement. Hawkers leap up and upset their tray loads of pens, mirrors, flashlights, etc. People run helter-skelter. The bus queue scatters. I see all this and decide it is safest in the middle of the road; traffic has been halted at the signals. The rat deprived of its human shield makes a dash across the road. The crows follow it like a swarm of bees. The rat turns to me for protection. It seeks shelter between my feet, then tries to clamber up my trousers. I yell and leap into the air like a dancing dervish. The rat falls on my foot, fat and clammy like a snake. I scream some more and run through speeding cars and buses back to the pavement. The rat and his tormentors disappear into the High Court.

'Arrey, what kind of Sardarji are you? You get scared of a mouse!' taunts a fellow back in the line for his bus. The entire queue bursts into peals of laughter. I am very angry. I want to tell him that it was not a mouse (chooha) but a rat. That I may be scared of little mice but not of rats like him. I scour my memory for the Hindustani word for rat, Hindi word for rat, Punjabi word for rat. There is no Indian word for a rat as distinct from a mouse. I resume my journey.

(1970)

The word 'sharaab' is derived from the Persian 'aab' for water and 'sharr' mischief, hence the water of mischief. Prophet Muhammad condemned it; the Quran denounces it as haraam—but holds out promise to the faithful that they will have plenty of it in Paradise with houris thrown in. Almost all my Muslim friends, men and women, Indian and Pakistani, can't wait to die but continue to enjoy their drinks while on earth.

They may ask:

Jannat mein ja kar tahooran peeogay
To yahaan peena kyon gunaah ho gaya?
Vahaan hoorein milney ka hai hukum,
Yahaan kyon zinah ka gunaah ho gaya?

If drinking will be legal in Paradise
Why is it declared on earth a crime?
If virgins are provided in Paradise
Why is womanizing on earth declared a crime?

Hinduism has an ambivalent attitude towards drinking. Madira, sura or somras were ingredients of the cocktail the gods churned out of the ocean. Ancient Sanskrit texts list eleven kinds of hard liquor of which three were top favourites of our ancestors—one distilled from the mahua flower (*Madhuca indica*), one made of honey like the English mead and one made from gur. These were often offered to the gods. Some yogi orders prescribe the use of liquor to enhance mystical experiences.

Wine is used in Jewish and Christian religious rituals. It is forbidden by Jain and Buddhist religious tenets. However, love of liquor overcame all religious taboos and attempts by governments to enforce prohibition. Neither Mahatma Gandhi nor Morarji Desai succeeded in persuading their countrymen that drinking liquor was harmful and impoverished families. Aldous Huxley rightly pointed out that more people lose their lives to drink than they do in wars fought for their country, king or the church.

Drinking in moderation creates social bonding. Drinking in excess creates social problems. A drunk man is a sorry sight. He becomes garrulous and aggressive before he passes out. A woman drinking to excess is pitiable. She becomes maudlin and loses the will to say no to men who make advances. A lady poet summed up her plight:

I like to have a martini,
Two at the very most.
After three I'm under the table,
After four I'm under my host.

I envy men who can drink endlessly but never get drunk. One such was the eminent Urdu poet Faiz Ahmed Faiz. He could drink from morning to late in the night without showing any traces of drunkenness. Another was the calligraphist Sadequain who made beautiful floral reproductions of the verses of the Quran after putting a bottle of hard liquor in his stomach. As for miserable me, I like two or three in the evening; more makes me groggy. However, I mean to enjoy my modest intake for the rest of my life.

Justice Narula has not given up his endeavour to make me a teetotaller. Being a god-fearing and kindly man with a silver white beard flowing down to his navel, I have no doubt he will have a luxury apartment booked for him in Paradise. I am equally certain I will be consigned to the fires of hell. I hope once in a while he will visit me and bring with him as gifts what he disdains—some good liquor and a couple of houris.

(2001)

CELEBRATING OLD AGE

This April two of my oldest friends' birthdays were celebrated by their friends. One was the eminent painter-sculptor Bhabesh Sanyal. He turned one hundred. The other was the equally eminent educationist Prem Kirpal, who turned ninety-two on 30 April. Come to think of it, I don't know anyone else, friend or relation, who has held out as long. Bhabesh is an imperious, grandly bearded man who stands ramrod straight, wears no glasses, has no problems with hearing, memory or speech. His wife Sneh and daughter Amba are there to look after him. Prem, though eight years younger than Bhabesh, broke his hip bone a few years ago and spends most of his day either in his bed or in his armchair. He has also become hard of hearing. Being a bachelor, he has been spared a nagging wife and if his friends become too garrulous, he simply switches off his hearing aid. He continues to write poetry (his latest collection was released on his birthday), he keeps refreshing his memory by going over albums of old photographs, and has a lot of female admirers, including Rajmata Gayatri Devi who came all the way from Jaipur to felicitate him. And he enjoys his Scotch.

Being a hundred must give a person a feeling of loneliness. All your contemporaries have departed and there is not much to look forward to in life. Dr Margaret Murray in her autobiography *My First Hundred Years* put it nicely: 'At my age I stand, as it were, on a high peak alone. I have no contemporaries with whom I can exchange memories or views. But that very isolation gives me a less biased view of that vast panorama of human life which is spread before the eyes of a centenarian, still more when those eyes are the eyes of an archaeologist. It is true that much of the far distance is shrouded in cloud and mist, but every here and there the fog thins a little and one can see clearly the advance of mankind.'

The most appropriate birthday greeting for Bhabesh Sanyal is 'Stay in good health and enjoy yourself till the very end.'

For Prem Kirpal I have a good quotation from Frank Buxton,

once editor of the *Boston Herald,* from his memoirs, *At Ninety-six:*

> I never thought that I'd survive,
> That I'd contrive to stay alive
> and whoop it up at ninety-five.
> But, damn it all, I find that I've
> Increased the score
> To one year more
> Wow:
> And now, you know, it seems to me
> That even one full century
> Need not be necessarily
> A real impossibility.

(2001)

ON BEING ALONE BUT NOT LONELY

I cannot understand people who complain about being bored with life. They moan 'nothing to do, nowhere to go, no one to talk to. There is nothing worse than being alone.' I tell them, 'I like being alone but never feel lonely.' There is so much to read, write and see. I never seem to get enough of the world without people. What I find boring is humans, chiefly those who complain of being bored. I put up with them for a few minutes and then politely ask them to depart as I have more interesting things to do—by which I mean to be left alone. I don't think they mind my being blunt; if they do, I don't care. I will be the master of my time not them.

I have so many dates to keep. I come out to the garden at 6 a.m. A Himalayan barbet perches itself at the top of a fir tree and begins to wail. It is a bit of a ventriloquist. Its calls sound as if they are from a long distance, whereas it is only a few yards away from me. Another barbet somewhere far down in the valley responds. Wailing and counter-wailing goes on for almost five minutes. Barbets depart, koels take over. They are followed by crows, white-cheeked bulbuls, mynas, Shimla tits and a whole variety of tiny birds my aged eyes fail to identify. If you have eyes to see and ears to hear, there is not a dull moment in any garden. If there are no birds, lie back, gaze at the sky and watch the clouds float by overhead. Why are some going from north to south and others from south to north? Evidently, at different levels, winds move in different directions. Why do clouds assume different shapes and colours? Why are some dark, moisture-laden and bring rain, while others are like fluffs of dry cotton and simply float about?

(2002)

WHY BOTHER TO WORK HARD

During the years I was an editor of some journal or the other, I had to contend with people on my staff who had a very lackadaisical attitude towards the work assigned to them. Their motto was sab chalta hai. It used to get my hackles up. There was a very attractive and talented young lady who I had picked up myself in the hope that she would make her mark as a writer and a poet and bring credit to the *Illustrated Weekly of India.* After a few weeks of diligent work, she became slack: came late to the office, was slipshod in her work, went out for lunch for long hours with some admirer or the other, and was the first to leave—even before the office closed. I told her as gently as I could that she was not pulling her weight. She tossed her head disdainfully and replied, 'Cheh! Why do you get so worked up about small errors. Tomorrow whatever you or I write will be sold to the raddiwallah.' I lost my cool and spoke sharply, 'You say that once more, I will sack you.' She stormed out of my room daring me to do so. A few days later she again made a faux pas correcting proofs. When I reprimanded her, she repeated her formula of life, saying sab chalta hai. I lost my temper: all her looks and gifts were diminished in my eyes. I gave her an ultimatum as strongly as I could. 'Either resign by tomorrow or I will send a note to the management to order your dismissal.' She resigned. She could have made a name for herself. Hardly anyone knows about her today except as someone with great promise who came to nothing. But she is at peace with herself as a contented, fulfilled housewife. That is more than I can say for myself.

Should one really bother too much about what one has to do to earn one's living? If a modicum of work can earn enough for us to live in modest comfort, why should we strive for excellence? It is instilled in us from childhood that we should put our heart and soul into what we are doing, it becomes our dharma, our religion. The Bhagavad Gita exhorts us to put in our best without bothering about the fruit. The opposite point of view is spelt out in passages of Ecclesiastes in the Old Testament: 'Vanity of vanities, all is vanity. What profit has a man from all his labours in which he toils under the sun? One generation passes away and another generation comes; but the earth abides for ever.' It goes on to add: 'That which has been is that which will be, that which is done is what will be done, and there is nothing new under the sun.' It is true that little or nothing remains of our worldly toil: 'There is no remembrance of former things, nor will there be remembrance of things that are to come by those who will come after...all is vanity, and grasping for the wind.' The holy book assures us, 'The sleep of the labouring man is sweet whether he eats little or much, but the abundance of the rich will not permit him to sleep.' So why struggle hard to amass wealth? More disturbing is the statement that goodness has no reward nor wickedness any punishment. 'There is a just man who perishes in his righteousness; and there is a wicked man who prolongs life in wickedness.' The inevitable conclusion is relax and enjoy life. Says the holy book: 'I recommend enjoyment; because a man has nothing better under the sun than to eat, drink and be merry, for this will remain with him in his labour all the days of his life which god gives him under the sun… Go eat your bread with joy and drink your wine with a merry heart.' There is no guarantee that the deserving win the battle of life for 'the race is not to the swift, nor the battle to the strong, nor bread to the wise, nor riches to men of understanding, nor favour to men of skill, but time and chance happen to them all.'

The choice is yours to make: If you strive for excellence, your only reward may be the satisfaction of knowing you did your best, or if you say why bother, it will make no difference.

(2002)

GOOD LIFE—THE ONLY RELIGION

Among the many bad habits I have, I have one or two good ones I can recommend to my readers. I have my own book of quotations. No item is taken from quotation books which are a dime a dozen. My quotations are compiled from books I have read or from letters I have received. Most of them are from Urdu poets. I also have some Sanskrit, Hindi, Punjabi and English quotations—in that order. When I have nothing better to do, I go over them. I was doing that when I discovered that the largest number deal with religion and hypocrisy, the two go very well together. Then came love, erotica and the pleasure of drinking. Why so much religion on the mind of an avowed agnostic? Because there is much hypocrisy that runs parallel with every one of them. As Thomas Fuller said: 'A good life is the only religion.' What is a good life? Ingersoll put it in simple words: 'Happiness is the only good life, the place to be happy is here, the time to be happy is now, the way to be happy is to help others.' Notice that God, prayer, places of worship find no mention for the simple reason that instead of uniting people, they divide them. Hence, Ella Wheeler Wilcox's summing up:

So many gods, so many creeds,
So many paths that wind and wind,
While just the art of being kind
Is all that the sad world needs.

The latest discovery I have made in my personal collection of quotations were a few lines from G. K. Chesterton which I had overlooked many times. They need to be read carefully and pondered over:

To love means loving the unlovable,
To forgive means forgiving the unpardonable,
Faith means believing the unbelievable,
Hope means hoping when everything is hopeless.

(2003)

IRRITATION, ANGER, RAGE

All the three are different stages of the same phenomenon we call anger. It starts with irritation (chirchirapan—khichh, khichh) develops into anger (gussa) and explodes into a rage (prakop). It is the second on the list of cardinal sins in Indian tradition: kama (lust), krodh (anger), lobh (greed), moh (attachment) and ahankar (arrogance). More than the other four, it is krodh which destroys relationships, sets sons and daughters against their parents, causes animosity between siblings, breaks up marriages and lifelong friendships, leads to quarrels and fisticuffs, raises one's blood pressure and brings on strokes.

One thing common to these five cardinal sins is that they are curable. You don't have to consult a doctor or go to a chemist to get a pill to get the better of your libido, desire or exaggerated self-esteem. You are your best doctor and can treat yourself without drugs of any kind. All you need is to become aware of these failings, think about the harm they have done to you and resolve to get rid of them.

However, there may be biological reasons for short-temperedness. When a child throws tantrums, his parents try to discover what causes them. Some children are more likely than others to fly off the handle, get into fights with their siblings or schoolmates. This may be caused by some stomach or brain malfunction. Parents are advised to have them medically checked up and once they have been cleared, counsel them on how to control their temper and warn them of the price they have to pay for not doing so. Thereafter every adult owes it to himself or herself to undertake this exercise themselves. Some problems may persist in later life. The lady I dedicated my second novel to would lose her temper with me without any provocation. I dropped her from my life. So did many of her other friends and admirers. Later we learnt she had a tumour in her brain which ultimately took her life. By then it was too late to make amends.

I have some more observations on the subject. Ill temper usually goes with authority. In families it is the monopoly of the parents, mainly the father. In school and college it is teachers who vent their ire against students; in jobs bosses against their underlings. Judges can be short-tempered with lawyers appearing before them, lawyers have to suffer their rudeness and wait till they are elevated to the bench before they can talk down to lawyers. Ministers of government can be brusque and tick off people working under them or anyone who crosses their path. Can you imagine Sahib Singh Verma, a lowly-paid librarian of a school, abusing the crew of a flight? At one time he could not have afforded air travel. But as minister he became arrogant and rude towards people who could not hit back. See the same Sahib Singh Verma bowing low as he namaskars the prime minister. I used to see Krishna Menon behave the same way. When Prime Minister Nehru came to London for a conference, Menon was all over him, carrying his overcoat and briefcase and sir-ing him. No sooner was he back in India House than he was ticking off members of the staff, throwing files at them and shouting at them to get out.

I worked with Krishna Menon and many others like him who tended to be more ill-tempered in the mornings than in the afternoons. It may have had something to do with bad digestion or poor flow of gastric juices. Too much alcohol in the evening can also make one short-tempered. Perhaps some doctor could enlighten us.

I have no specific remedies for bad temper besides becoming aware of it and keeping one's mouth shut till it has subsided. Silence is the most powerful antidote to krodh. Swallow it with your spittle, never put it in words.

(2003)

THE IMPORTANCE OF BATHING

At different periods of history different people had different notions of the importance of bathing. Indians must be the only people who made a daily bath an essential religious ritual. After clearing one's bowels the next thing one has to do is to take a bath. No bath, no breakfast. No bath, no entering a temple or a gurdwara. Sikh practice puts bath (ishnaan) on a par with prayer (naam) and charity (daan). Bathing in rivers, notably the Ganga, washes off sins. Likewise, Sikh ritual prescribes a bath in the sarovar (sacred tank) along a gurdwara as a spiritual cleanser. The most important sarovar is the one in the middle of which stands Harmandir, the Golden Temple. The tank was dug by Guru Ramdas, the fourth guru. The incantation which goes with the holy dip runs:

> Guru Ramdas sarovar nhaatey
> Sab utrey paap kamaatey
>
> Bathe in the holy tank of Guru Ramdas
> and all sins you have committed will be washed away.

I have accumulated a lot of sins but never yet washed them off in any sacred tank or holy river. I also discovered through experience that a hot bath during winter months often gave me a cold and I could clean myself just as well by rubbing my body with a damp towel. My college years in England changed my attitude towards bathing. Like other Indians, I believed that wallowing in a long bath tub in your own body's dirt was unhealthy. After some months, I came to the conclusion that an English bath was far more cleansing than pouring water over oneself with a lota. So, during winter, I bathed only twice a week. And was none the dirtier for it.

During my stint in Paris, I discovered that most French homes did not have a bathroom. Instead, they used a contraption called a bidet on which they sat astride as on a horse and turned on a tap which shot a shower of warm water into their bottoms and genitals. This, repeated after soaping their private parts, did quite a thorough job. The French sponged their armpits and liberally sprinkled them with talcum powder. A proper body wash was a weekend ritual performed in a public bath. Most Saturdays, girls from the office where I worked spent an hour or more in these public baths and were ready for a prolonged weekend with their boyfriends. When I rented a house in a suburb of Paris I had to have a bathroom installed.

Europeans have an interesting history of bathing. Long before they turned Christian, Scandinavians and Germans bathed naked in lakes and rivers during the summer months, and in public baths during the winter. With the advent of Christianity nakedness came to be associated with vulgarity, lascivious thoughts and, therefore, sinful. St Agnes never took a bath; St Margaret never washed herself; Pope Clement III issued an edict forbidding bathing or even wetting one's face on Sundays. Between the sixteenth and eighteenth centuries, the practice of bathing in rivers was frowned upon. In 1736 in Baden, Germany, the authorities issued a warning to students against 'the vulgar, dangerous and shocking practice of bathing'.

Slowly, very slowly, prejudice against nudity and bathing abated. Nudist clubs sprang up. Sunbathing in the nude became fashionable. Today, at any seaside in Europe, Canada, Australia or New Zealand you will see men, women and children strolling along beaches as naked as the day they were born. And bathing together in the nude does not shock anyone except those who still regard nudity as a sin. Having a bath everyday has become common practice now.

I am reminded of an exchange of words in the British House of Commons in the early years of World War II. A Labour minister in charge of power was pleading that a lot of coal could be saved if it was not used to heat water for bathing and a bath a week was good enough. Winston Churchill stood up and remarked, 'No wonder the Labour Party is in such bad odour.'

(2001)

WHAT IS LOVE?

It is easier to say what it is not than what it is. Even after you have excluded emotions that have nothing to do with it, you are up against many kinds of love which have little in common. You may love your God, your country and your parents but you'll sense that there is a qualitative difference between these kinds of love and the love that envelops a man and a woman of somewhat the same age and capable of sexual intercourse. Dorothy Tennov, an American psychiatrist, has defined this kind of love as 'an obsessive, all-embracing passion for another person that strikes seemingly from nowhere and makes life a hell of uncertainty, punctuated by brief moments of ecstasy'. She has given this brand of man-woman fixation the name 'limerence'.

Tennov's definition of love is as good as I have seen anywhere but it does not explain why this 'obsessive, all-embracing passion' erupts, why it loses intensity and why it often turns to sour hate.

How and why two people of the opposite sex are attracted to each other to the exclusion of others has never been fully explored. The urge is without doubt physical because it usually manifests itself on the approach of puberty. It is also often entirely a yearning of the body without any mental or emotional overtones. Both males and females pass through such a period when compulsions of the body are so explosive that they will seek their fulfilment through the most readily available persons without the slightest affection for them. This is lust not love. Love is more subtle than lust and while lust can be fulfilled by expending the lust, love has more frustration than fulfilment.

Why two people fall in love with each other can only be explained by probing their psyches. It is believed that most people fall in love with people very much like themselves. This has been confirmed by computer matings. If it is so, we can presume that there is a strong element of narcissism in a person's choice. It has been noticed that many couples in love resemble each other like brother and sister. But, as often, a couple totally unlike each other in their physical makeup are strongly drawn towards each other. This may be explained as the negative aspect of narcissism.

It is apparent that love is initially stirred by physical attraction and is born in the eye. It is on the physical that the mental and emotional relationship is built. Even the emotional is frequently reinforced by appeals which are essentially physical: 'You are the most beautiful person in the world etc.' Love is not man's quest for an idealized Helen; it is elevating a girl who is available to 'Hellenistic' heights. That is why men do not roam the world looking for the girl of their dreams but weave them round the girl next door. She is there, others are not. This phenomenon has been given the label 'equity': in love people get what they deserve. However idealized the love may become, its consummation is in the act of sex. As Donne put it in his earthy way:

> Whoever loves, if he do not propose
> The right true end of love,
> he's one that goes
> To sea for nothing but to make him sick

The romantic edifice of love has to have sex as its foundation stone. Once that is gone, love becomes something else: companionship, friendship. Or whatever else. The circumstances in which a couple meet each other often compel them to fall in love. The same couple in a different setting might not even notice each other. In one of her novels, Rosamond Lehmann narrates how two children who happened to be playing together by the seaside saw a flock of geese swoop down through a misty sky to land on the sea in front of them. When they met again many years later they promptly fell in love because of the mystic experience they had shared in their childhood. I have little doubt that if an Indian mountaineer getting on top of Everest from the Indian side were to meet a Chinese lass coming up from the other, they would immediately fall in love. And not in the Hindi-Chini-bhai-bhai or the bhai-behen way.

American researchers have further discovered that a man in an excitable state is more prone to fall in love than when he is calm and placid. Apparently, excitement causes chemical changes in his blood and brain vessels which make him more receptive to emotional stimuli.

High altitude brings about similar effects. Hence, the high incidence of marriage between air hostesses and passengers. The Americans have further established that the traumatic experience of rejection induces hunger for certain types of compensatory diet like chocolate.

Speaking from personal experience, I can say that all this theorizing about love is hogwash. People fall in and out of love all the time in all kinds of places and make the most impossible combinations. There is nothing exclusive about love because people can be in love with varying degrees of intensity with many people at the same time. I do not know if other people suffer anguish when they are rejected; I feel an exhilarating sense of release.

(1980)

ABOLISH MARRIAGE?

I have always believed that the institution of marriage implying an exclusive, lifelong (till death do us part) arrangement is contrary to nature, and man-made laws enforcing monogamy corrode the personalities of both man and wife.

Since few people have the courage to break their marriages because of social censure or lethargy, I suggest a change in the law whereby all marriages would be compulsorily dissolved every five years and the parties be asked to decide whether they wished to remarry each other or someone else—or resume the state of single blessedness. The main hurdle in this scheme of things is the upbringing of children because children need both parents for their mental and physical health. The closest human society has come to in resolving this problem are the kibbutzim in Israel where married couples perform their respective daily tasks in fields or offices, while their children are taken care of by specially qualified nurses and doctors. Parents have constant access to their children and are free to take them home if they so desire. To the best of my knowledge the kibbutz-reared children do not suffer the scars that children of quarrelling parents or broken homes suffer and grow up to be healthy, normal citizens.

Recent research on sexuality and the rearing of offspring conducted by Richard Leakey and Roger Lewin (*People of the Lake*) gives fresh insight into the motives which bring males and females of a species together and their attitudes towards the rearing of their offspring. They trace it back to the origin of life and the desire to perpetuate their species. The authors maintain that, contrary to popular belief, the male and female after they have performed their respective sexual roles, do their best to ditch their partners and leave them to look after the offspring. This was simpler when life was confined to water. Female frogs laid eggs in floating gelatinous blobs, male frogs squirted their sperm on them and neither was saddled with looking after their offspring as the resultant tadpoles fended for themselves. But the problem of survival became acute when life came to the land. Female birds had to produce eggs with protective shells and often both parents were required to hatch, feed and protect their offspring from predators. To this day the highest incidence (90 per cent) of monogamous unions is found amongst birds. But usually they only last one courtship-breeding season.

The evolution of humans from monkeys, their search for food from hunting, through agriculture to organized society was responsible for the many biological changes that took place in their anatomy. In the animal world, females came into heat at specified periods when they could conceive and in turn rouse the sexual instincts of their males. It is only amongst humans that the female is always ready for sex and the male always ready to give it to her. 'In all probability,' say the authors, 'heightened human sexuality evolved as emotional cement to an economic contract in which the product is children. In other words, sex became sexy for humans—particularly for females—as an essential ingredient in the uniquely interdependent child-rearing band of *Homo sapiens*.'

The authors throw further light on other interesting phenomena, such as women should be more fussy than men in choosing their sexual partner and that they should look for someone who will be socially and economically successful; men are more naturally adulterous than women; female prostitution should be more common than male prostitution; men are likely to be more severe with adulterous wives than wives will be with husbands who seek illicit sex elsewhere; that the coupling of older men with young women should be more common than the reverse; that the maternal grandmother is more certain about her genetic investment in her daughter's children than is a paternal grandmother and will therefore be more solicitous in offering help in caring for the infants; that under favourable economic circumstances men will seek to be polygamous, and that such circumstances are likely to be more common than those conducive to polyandry; that the significant difference in body size between men and women implies that in our recent history men competed with each other for more than their fair share of desirable women; and that monogamy is not the natural state of humankind.

It would seem that man's genetic animal past is at variance with his present attempt to concede equal rights to women. But the future is with women. She may have to bear children for millennia to come but with all the new baby foods available, she no longer has to give them nourishment. Her bosom having no alimentary purpose to serve may in due course shrivel to the size of the male nipple and become a shrunk relic of the past. What male would like to live in a world of bosomless females! Not I.

(1979)

MY EXPERIMENTS WITH MY BODY

Are you fat and forty? Dyspeptic and constipated? Uptight, overworked and losing your virility? Don't despair. You can still shed your spare tyre, regain those rock hard muscles, and feel ready to take on half the population of the world—the female half!

I am not sure at what age I became consciously concerned with my body. Certainly not as a child. In adolescence I became aware of its many shortcomings. I was not as tall as I would like to have been. I was squat, short-necked and prone to put on fat in the wrong places. I wanted to be an athlete: a long-distance runner, a tennis champion and a hockey ace. I wanted to build my muscles and become a Bharat Shri. Much as I tried I could not achieve any of these ambitions. A severe attack of typhoid fever followed by two relapses left my intestines in very poor shape. When I recovered from the fever I discovered that my digestive system had been seriously impaired. Almost everything I liked to eat disagreed with me. I suffered from indigestion, flatulence and constipation. And as usual with people with a bad stomach I became prone to many ailments. Migraine was a monthly affair. One cold followed another; catarrh became chronic and often made my life a misery. I was often reminded of the Arabic proverb: 'He who has health has hope; he who has hope has everything.' I had lost both health and hope.

In middle age I learnt to enjoy alcohol; just any kind of alcohol. The years in the diplomatic and international civil service where cocktails, wines and spirits were de rigueur with every meal (and in between meals) played havoc with my system. I consulted all kinds of doctors, hakims and vaids. What they prescribed gave me relief—but only for short durations. Following Voltaire's advice that everyone should be his own physician, I decided to examine my body, make my own diagnosis and take myself in hand.

I had always believed in strenuous exercise. I had no patience with yoga which I found very boring. Besides, exertion that did not make me sweat out the poison in my system and leave me pleasantly exhausted was not my concept of exercise. Consequently though I had reconciled myself to being a second-rater in sports I continued to indulge in vigorous tennis, hockey and squash.

Outwardly I managed to look fitter than most men of my age. For my inner ailments I sought the advice of a naturopath. I was then in my middle forties and living in London. Dr Leif, an Austrian, ran a nature-cure clinic in sylvan Hertfordshire about thirty miles from London. He had converted an old country manor called Champneys into a kind of hospital-cum-rest house. This had become the subject of much humour; the inmates were usually referred to as 'Leif's loonies' or 'Champney's chimps'. I joined this 'lunatic' group.

I was examined by Dr Leif—my heart, blood pressure, urine, stool etc., and pronounced fine. I then told him of internal problems. He invited me to have all my meals with him. I was to eat and drink what I did every day. Alongside my seat at the dining table he placed a large glass bowl. Into this bowl he poured the equivalent of everything I consumed: morning cups of tea; the egg, bacon, toast and coffee I took for breakfast; cups of mid-morning coffee; cocktails and lunch; afternoon tea; whisky, steak, vegetables with the appropriate wines followed by coffee and cognac. Then we retired for a chat by the fireside. He brought the glass bowl full of the slop along. By then the food and alcohol had fermented and bubbles were popping out of it. He weighed the stuff in my presence and asked me to smell it. It was foul and weighed over a couple of kilos. All he said to me was, 'If you stuff all this into yourself every day, how do you expect your poor body to cope with it?' The message went home. The only treatment he prescribed was fifteen days of fasting followed by a week of instructions about what to eat.

I discovered that before undertaking a fast the stomach must be thoroughly cleansed, otherwise the body tends to absorb the festering food that is in it. This can have deleterious effects. I was put through what was known as a 'colonic irrigation'. A penis-sized gadget with two tubes was inserted into my rectum. One tube pumped in warm water, the other sucked it out along with the contents of the stomach. I wondered what pleasure homosexuals got out of buggery. However, this was followed by an oil massage and a vigorous rubbing of salt. By the end of the morning I was thoroughly exhausted.

Although I felt as clean as the proverbial whistle, I was ravenously hungry. 'Lunch' consisted of a single orange. 'Tea' was a glass of tepid water spiked with honey. 'Dinner' another orange. For the next few days I dreamt of nothing but my favourite dishes. There were a number of pretty starlets who sprawled about the lawns taking the sun in complete nudity. They did not interest me one bit. A juicy, well-done steak with a bottle of Mâcon followed by a ton of ice cream topped with hot chocolate sauce was what I craved far more than sex. But all I got were two oranges and lots of hot water. And a few more colonic irrigations. On the fourth day there was a humming in my ears. Two days later the humming disappeared. So did the craving for food. I shed many kilos of fat without any discomfort.

The ordeal came to an end. I was broken back into the food habit with a bowl of yoghurt which took me a long time to eat. It was followed by salad and uncooked vegetables.

An amusing incident which sticks in my mind concerned two inmates of Champneys. One was a tailor from Leeds. He was a man of gigantic proportions and had an unquenchable thirst for liquor. Three weeks of fasting and abstinence from alcohol had knocked out most of his fat. He proudly displayed the gap between his trousers and his now shrunken belly. Three days before he was due to leave he succumbed to the temptation of taking out one of the starlets (likewise hungry and thirsty) to a pub.

The effect of liquor on their cleansed stomachs was lethal. When the pub closed they bought themselves a bottle of gin and decided to spend the night together. Despite the bouts of sex they were uproariously drunk in the morning. The staff put them through colonic irrigations, massages, ice water douches. All to no avail. When Dr Leif came to hear of the gross violation of rules (drinking, not sex) he reprimanded them in front of all the other patients and ordered them out of the institution. Neither of them was in the least bit repentant. 'All this bloody fasting was worth this one night,' roared the tailor. They left Champneys arm in arm.

When I returned to London I had trouble with my eyes and had to consult an optician. I was pleasantly surprised to learn that my glasses needed changing because my eyesight had improved.

Nothing made me more conscious of my body than those three weeks amongst Leif's loonies. Thereafter, I began to be selective of the food I ate and watched my weight every day. Migraines disappeared. The colds became less frequent. All I did to avoid them was to take cold baths throughout the winter and an occasional tablet of Vitamin C. (Dr Linus Pauling, twice Nobel Laureate says that Vitamin C is the only answer to the common cold.)

I developed an unpleasant trait of mocking people with paunches. I recall telling the then somewhat corpulent General Kulwant Singh that if I were the defence minister I would sack any soldier who had a paunch. He rudely ordered me out of his office. To an assembly of Sikhs who were critical of my unorthodox ways, I retorted by saying that anyone who was physically unfit had no business to call himself a Sikh. Hadn't Guru Gobind Singh exhorted: 'Khalsa sada rahey kanchan keya kal na kabhoon byapai (Let your body be like burnished gold).'

No ills will ever befall it. Indians in their forties should be particularly careful with their bodies. The burden of the country rests heavily on the shoulders of the university-educated and the affluent who form a very small proportion of the population of the country. It is in the forties that they usually come to the top of their professions or other businesses. And it is in the forties that they begin to indulge themselves in more food and drink than is necessary for them, keep indifferent hours, take less exercise and usually begin to suffer from ailments like ulcers, piles, high blood pressure, etc., which take a heavy toll of their efficiency and eventually kill them.

It is in the forties and the fifties that they must, if they have not learnt before, control their diet and take exercise. The moral is that a rich man who wants to be healthy must learn to live like a poor man. If they do not do so, they will only murder themselves and be guilty of homicide in the second degree. A simple rule for diet was prescribed by the Talmud: one third of the stomach should have food, one third drink and the remaining third should be empty. It should be borne in mind that more people die of overeating and drinking than are killed in wars.

Danny Kaye, the celebrated comedian who I happened to be interviewing over All India Radio, told me the secret of his youthful vitality (he was seventy-five, looked fifty-five and was agile as a panther). 'I take a little exercise,' he said, 'it takes no more than a few seconds twice a day. You do it; you'll remain fit all your life.'

'A few seconds twice a day?' I asked in disbelief. 'What kind of exercise is that?'

'At lunch and at dinner when I am offered a second helping I waggle my head to indicate no.'

The guiding principle should be to eat little and eat right. Everyone should carefully watch what kinds of food disagree with him and rigorously eliminate them from his diet. I find milk and milk products (except dahi) make me sluggish or bilious. Cakes, pastries—all kinds of sweets give me flatulence. So do highly spiced things like chaat or bhel. Whenever I indulge in them, the self-generated gas in the stomach makes me like a jet plane. Others take all these in their stride but are upset by meat, eggs or saag.

It is best to prepare your own menu—keeping in mind that it must ensure regular, easy evacuation. A constipated stomach is an invitation to disease. You will notice that if the stomach is not clean, even a mild toothache will be aggravated, athlete's foot becomes more itchy and dandruff erupts in your scalp.

Living in Bombay for nine years, I rarely used my car. I walked to the office and back every day. I reduced my lunch to a bowl of soup or yoghurt and fruit. I continued playing tennis—usually mixed doubles where I combined exercise with some mild flirtation.

I also joined the Taj Health Club. It was the hours spent at the club and discussions with the director, Mrs Rama Bans, which convinced me that everyone who can afford it should join a health club. This lady, a grandmother in her fifties, has the face of a young woman in her thirties. She made a diet chart for me; 'Control your intake of calories and you will not put on an extra ounce,' she said. And so it was. One extra drink, one extra helping of a sweet dish and it showed on the weighing machine the next day. I learnt to miss a meal to compensate for the overindulgence of the day before.

At the Taj Health Club in Bombay there was an assortment of

members hoping for different kinds of benefits. There were film stars and obese Gujarati ladies only interested in shedding weight; there were men both young and old who wanted to become more potent. And there were business executives who just wanted to get rid of their tensions and relax. I believe in certain measure all of them got what they were looking for.

Health clubs in our five-star hotels are expensive affairs. But much cheaper than doctors and medicine bills. And if used regularly they cost no more than five rupees per day which is less than the cost of the hot water, soap, towels, talcum powder, etc., which are consumed. There is no better place for studying your body and rectifying things that have gone wrong than a health club. It keeps a record of your weight, girth, blood pressure. The slightest deviation is noticed and you will be told what to do about it.

Since most men and women who frequent health clubs are in their middle years and unable to play strenuous games, the gymnasium provides them gentler ways of exercising. A yoga instructor is always available for personal guidance; there are yoga classes for those who wish to do them en masse. The gymnasium is equipped with a variety of gadgets. The electric belt and cycle to tone up the muscles. The whirlpool with jets of hot water which if directed to parts of the body you wish to reduce can be most beneficial. Then there is the sauna or the steam bath followed by immersion in a chilled pool. You sweat it out in an overheated room, the icy water gives a pleasant jolt to the system. Every session of this hot-cold immersion has to be followed by a few minutes of rest on a flat wooden bench. The sense of relaxation is blissful. An oil massage once a week tones up the body and squeezes tensions out of the system like water squeezed out of a sponge. At the end of an hour or two in the health club, you feel as light as a feather. As I put it in my vulgar lingo, you'll feel like taking on half the population of the world—the female half. The evening drink goes down better, the food tastes tastier and you sleep the sleep of the just.

Many famous men have written a lot of rubbish about health. Someone has said that people who spend most of their time watching their health have little time to enjoy it. It is true that concern with health should not become an obsession and there should be a certain amount of calculated carelessness about it. But it cannot be argued that it must take top priority in everyone's scale of values. When Jonathan Swift prescribed Dr Diet, Dr Quiet and Dr Merriman as the three best doctors in the world, what he meant was that you yourself must watch your food, teach yourself the art of quiet solitude—and cheerfulness will follow as the night the day.

(1980)

AN UNFULFILLED DREAM

The world has begun to depress me. It may be that in twilight years I have abandoned the zest for living I once had and am preparing myself for the night of which I know nothing and the promised dawn in which I do not believe. On further self-analysis I am convinced that my depression is not entirely due to any morbid forethoughts of my demise. It is more due to the shattering of the dreams of my youth that the world has become a depressing place.

In my younger days, I dreamt that within a matter of a decade or two, people would be free, there would be no tensions between nations and no wars, everyone would have enough to eat, drink and live in comfort; gifted men and women would enrich our lives with good books, pictures, music and dance. For some time, things seemed to move in that direction. Many nations attained independence and began to settle their problems by talking to each other, we overcame most diseases, began to produce more food and made life worth living. All that remained to be done was to free the human race from the bondage of racial prejudice and religious bigotry and create an atmosphere in which people in power would not try to impose their views on their fellow citizens.

Alas! Racial prejudice not only continued as it was in the medieval ages but even erupted in the most virulent form in a state which I hoped would set an example to other nations on how to treat their racial minorities. The Soviet treatment of Jews is an even more sinister development than the treatment of blacks in South Africa or Rhodesia. Being an agnostic, I looked forward to a world where the new generation would free itself of the mumbo jumbo of archaic religious practices and yet be truthful, helpful and decent towards each other. Religion too has re-erupted in different forms all over the globe. Catholics fight Protestants, Copts fight Muslims, Muslims fight Jews.

Presidents Carter and Reagan quote the Bible at each other. Heads of Muslim states find it necessary to proclaim they are Muslims. In

Pakistan, General Zia-ul-Haq reintroduces the chopping of limbs and flogging in public. No one protests.

I take a look at my own country. Our new rulers tell us that we are going back to Gandhi—whatever that means. In effect all they are doing is to use Gandhi as a broom to sweep away Nehru. The Punjab is ruled by Akali zealots. Many other states are also ruled by equally zealous Hindu bigots sporting caste marks on their foreheads. Muslim friends advise me that if I mean to retain my image as a friend of the Muslims, I must not write anything critical pertaining to their Personal Law—including polygamy and the lesser status that their women (in comparison to others) have now been relegated to. The cow is once again sacred (to me so are other animals, particularly cats and dogs) and liquor is the worst form of poison. All these are beyond argument. This is not the India I dreamt of forty years ago. And I find it utterly depressing.

(1977)

GOD & HIS MESSENGERS

'Panditji was undoubtedly attracted towards me with what I said and, I admit, with my appearance...if he had married anyone I am sure it would have been me... But there was never any question about it. What Mathai has written is a lie.'

There is more to Shraddha Mata than the Nehru connection.

Four funeral pyres ablaze, a fifth corpse in a white shroud surrounded by women wailing and beating their breasts. The acrid smell of burning flesh. And in the midst of this macabre setting, Shraddha Mata reclining on a wood takhtposh calmly telling the beads of her rosary. This was in Delhi's Nigambodh Ghat. She, a tantric sanyasin, was performing a mahakal yagna. Graveyards and cremation grounds are regarded as particularly suitable for such rites.

Shraddha Mata is a short, somewhat corpulent lady in her mid-sixties (b. 1917). She wears thick-lensed glasses to read; when she takes them off you can see that she is a handsome woman who must have been quite a beauty in her younger days. As they say: ruins proclaim the glory of the monument that once was. Even today her fair skin is unwrinkled, her bosom full, her talk animated and her speech blunt: it is always tu not aap—and yet her words exude affection.

'Kaun?' she demanded as I turned the flap of the gunnysack curtain she had put around her little temporary ashram in the cremation ground.

'It is me. I have come for your darshan,' I replied.

'You must have a name, what is it?'

I announced my name.

'Baithja,' she said, pointing to the bare floor beside her wooden couch.

As I lowered myself, my feet touched a pair of pink plastic slippers.

'Arrey kaisa admi hai tu!—what kind of a man are you? You put your feet on a sanyasin's sandals!'

I apologized.

She peered into my face and asked, 'Are you the same fellow who was editor of the *Illustrated Weekly*?'

I admitted I was.

'Why did they sack you?'

I explained as best as I could.

'Why have you come to see me?'

'Darshan'—and since I could not think of the correct Hindi word, I used the English, 'aur thodi curiosity.'

'Arrey chhod curiosity, phuriosity!' she snorted with a kindly laugh. 'You must have read what that fellow Mathai has written about me and Pandit Nehru. You want to write the same kind of bakwas—rubbish.'

I gave her my word of honour that I would not write anything she did not approve of, and not even bring up the topic of her association with Panditji if she did not want me to do so. But I said I would like to know more about her, why had she renounced the world and become a sanyasin. What had she got out of it?

She listened quietly as she told the beads of her rosary. After a while she spoke: 'I have read some of your writings. Are you a nastik?' I admitted I was an agnostic.

'You do not believe in Ishwara?'

'No, Mataji, I do not believe in anything I know nothing about.'

'You seem to be an arrogant man—ghamandi.'

I protested, 'No, Mataji, I have no ghamand. I only plead ignorance of what I do not know. Maybe you have seen Ishwara and can tell me something about him.'

She promptly cut me down to size: 'Arrey ja! You have still to learn the alphabet aa ee uu and you want me to teach you the Vedas! Get rid of your coat-patloon, get into a loincloth, sit at my feet for a few years and I will teach you about God. You have a little twig before your eyes which prevents you from seeing the Sun. I will remove that twig and you will see this entire drishti—cosmos is Ishwara.' Thus, ended the first seance. 'Come again if you wish' were her parting words.

Something, I do not know what, compelled me to return to Nigambodh Ghat the next evening. The 'welcome' was as blunt as the first.

'Tu phir aa gaya—you have come again?' she demanded.

'You asked me to do so,' I replied.

'Baith.'

I took my seat beside her takhtposh.

'I believe that Mathai has again written something about me in his second book. What has he said?'

I told her that he had written about her association with Pandit Nehru some time in 1948-49, the birth of a son in a Catholic institution in Bangalore, her abandoning the child after a few days, the recovery and destruction of the letters Panditji is said to have written her. She heard me out without interrupting me and made a non-committal comment. 'I warned Panditji then that he should not trust Mathai; he was the kind of viper who would bite him after his death.'

The second seance was followed by a third and a fourth. The Delhi Municipal Corporation ousted her from Nigambodh Ghat. She moved twenty miles away to Shiv Shambhu Dayal Mandir in the Okhla Industrial Estate. I sought her out in her new abode, this time determined to ask her life story. After some hesitation, she complied.

HER LIFE STORY

'I am not sure of my date of birth nor the name of the village in which I was born except that it was in Sultanpur district (UP). I was the only child of my mother. My father had taken a second wife and died a couple of months before I was born. I was given in adoption to my father's sister who was the Rani of Singhpur-Panhauna, a state near Ayodhya. This was done as the Rani had no child and my father had managed her estates.'

'What caste are you?

'Brahmin-Kshatriya—halfway between the two upper castes.'

'How did you get mixed up with religion—and sanyas?'

Shraddha Mata reclined on a bolster and after pondering for a while replied: 'I'll tell you all. My conversion to the sanyasi's way of life came in three successive stages. I was perhaps born with the desire because even as a child of five I was fascinated by sadhus and sanyasis. I began wearing gerua and refused to wear any other colour. Then I came across a statue of the Buddha in the meditation pose. I was captivated. I got a small figurine of the same and instead of playing with dolls as other girls of my age did, I always carried my Buddha on me. The third incident that made me finally decide to abandon the world I lived in came two years later when I was only seven years old. As in many landed families, I spent more time with the servants than with my adoptive mother. I was particularly close to the woman who had been my dhaya who I came to address as Bua. One evening she was taken ill and did not come to the house. The next morning I went to the servants' quarters. There she was laid on the ground, wrapped up in a shroud. I asked someone 'Where is my bua?' They replied, 'She has gone to Rama.' This created a veritable storm in my breast. I wanted to know who that Rama was and where had my bua gone to? As is customary in our part of India, poor Hindus bury their dead and place a charpoy upside down on the grave. I used to visit Bua's grave every day, through sun and rain, winter and summer till the charpoy had crumbled to bits and the grave was hardly recognizable. And every time I asked myself, "Where is Rama that my bua has gone to?" It was perhaps a year later when I was eight that I persuaded an old woman who was going on pilgrimage to Badrinath to take me along with her. I slipped out of the house unnoticed at midnight. Instead of going to the railway station where they were sure to look for me, we went along the Ganga and took the train from the next station.'

MARRIAGE

'The party of pilgrims returned to the village but I stayed in Badrinath for another six months. Ultimately my adoptive mother Rani Ragho Nath Koer bullied the old woman into telling her where I was and sent a party of men to fetch me. The Rani decided that the one way out for her was to marry me off to someone. I was only nine when she arranged my betrothal. Then real trouble began. My husband-to-be and I quarrelled all the time; we had bitter fights. This went on for over two years till that engagement was called off. I was then twelve or thirteen. Now my quarrels began with my Rani mother. Many times we went into sulks, refused to eat or talk to each other. I got so fed up that I decided to agree to anything that would get me out of the situation. There were lots of distant cousins who wanted to marry me—there was the property that I would inherit and I was regarded as good looking. Another marriage was quickly arranged. This was with another distant relative called Phanindra Pal Singh. I don't remember exactly whether he had done his Bar or was going to do it. But he was considered quite a catch. Even this marriage did not work out. My husband and his parents kept me under surveillance as if I was a prisoner. I wasn't even allowed to go to the toilet without a couple of maidservants watching me and an armed guard close by. It was not a marriage but a kind of death. Ultimately I wrote a letter to Gandhiji telling him that I belonged to a taluqdar family and had been forced into a marriage against my will. And that I wanted to become a sanyasin, join him to serve my country. I sent this letter through a cousin who was going to meet Gandhiji. A few days later I got a reply from Mahadeo Desai saying that Gandhiji had agreed to my joining him and I should come at once. Altogether I had spent no more than five to six weeks with my husband. Then I slipped away.'

'You seem uncommonly well-educated. But you have said nothing about your schooling.'

'Oh that! I had dozens of tutors at home. I was taught Sanskrit, Hindi, English, everything. I did not take any degrees because women in families like ours did not go to schools or college or sit for exams.'

Shraddha Mata resumed her narrative. 'I was with Gandhiji for forty days. My husband turned up to claim me and even showed Bapu our wedding picture. Gandhiji was very firm in his reply. He said, "I know of no taluqdar's daughter; I only know this girl who has come to me. She is like a wave of the Ganga and you cannot lock her up in a cage. Let her go." I stayed with Gandhiji till I was taken very ill. But by then I had become a free person.'

'How did you come by the name Shraddha Mata? Surely it was not the name given to you by your family?'

'I have had a variety of names. In my horoscope I am Parvati. My real name which was never used is Shyam Kala. At home everyone called me Bacchi Sahib. When I took sanyas I was given yet another name Sushriyananda Saraswati. But somehow it was Shraddha that stuck. I think I gave it to myself at Gandhiji's ashram. Shraddha is an abbreviation of Sat Ko Dharan—one who clasps the truth. Mata—

mother—came to be appended to it in later life.'

LADY OF THE FORT

This is all that I was able to elicit in the five evenings I spent with Shraddha Mata in Delhi. She invited me to visit her in Jaipur where she would give me whatever she had in the way of photographs of her earlier days and articles written on her. She promised, 'I will tell you what I have told no one else.' That was too tempting an invitation to let go. Ten days later, Raghu Rai and I flew into Jaipur.

Hathroi Fort, atop a rocky escarpment, broods over the city of Jaipur. Its topmost turret gives a spectacular view of the huddle of pink bazaars and beyond them to the range of hills crowned with other forts and palaces. Hathroi was designed to block an invader's path to Jaipur and Amber. It fell into desuetude and became the haunt of flying foxes, rock pigeons and sand lizards. In 1953, Maharaja Sawai Man Singh turned it over to Shraddha Mata. She converted the citadel into the headquarters of the Mahashakti Peeth. The lookout turret from which Rajput warriors had scanned the horizons to sight an approaching enemy is now occupied by a life-sized marble statue of a goddess. When the city of Jaipur sleeps, the goddess and her worshipper keep vigil. Shraddha Mata prays and meditates through the night into the early hours of the dawn.

We stride uphill to a massive gate and let ourselves in through a small aperture. An obese mongrel welcomes us with a happy bark and vigorous wagging of its tail. This is Bhairon; he is a Brahmachari dog who has been kept away from the temptations of sex by never being let out of the fortress. While Surendra Singh, Shraddha Mata's young secretary and acolyte, goes to announce our arrival, we take a look at the courtyard. It has a well in the centre; pigeons rest deep down its sides and fly out like bees from a hive. On one side is a pumpkin patch smelling of green leaves; against another wall is a marble statue of Shiva, a woman squats in front reciting jap out of a hymnal. Rising above the parapet of the well are the priests' quarters; their womenfolk are busy cooking the morning meal. Through a turning, twisting, perpetually shaded passageway a flight of broad stone stairs mounts skywards to the turret temple. Along the parapets on either side are Shraddha Mata's gufa and her 'reception rooms'. We take off our shoes and go up to greet her. 'First go and pay homage to the goddess, she will rid you of your nastikta and give shakti to your pen. Then come back to me.'

Shraddha Mata has a lot to say and drops broad hints that she may not have too long a time at her disposal to say it. Mathai's insinuations about the nature of her relationship continue to bother her. She denounces him as one of the 'anti-Hindu' group who conspired to create misunderstandings between her and the late Prime Minister. 'A good man continues to reform and become better till his last breath; an evil man remains evil till he dies,' she remarks. 'And what was it that I tried to instil into Nehru's mind? Only that India had a great spiritual tradition which must not be thrown away in the name of secularism. I believe in democracy, it liberates people from fear. But if you wish to preserve democracy you must replace the void created by the absence of fear by something positive, something spiritual which gives you a sense of responsibility and discipline. I call this adhyatmik samajvad, the nearest English equivalent is spiritual policy. Otherwise, the only alternative is the dandebazi of the MISA.'

I looked up my notes and asked her to resume the narrative of her life from the time she left Gandhiji's ashram. 'For the next three years or more I worked with the Harijan Sewak Sangh, organizing night schools in villages around Agra and in the Awadh region. My chief contacts were Thakkar Bappa and Acharya Jugal Kishore. This must have been between the sixteenth and nineteenth years of my life. Then I threw it all up and retired to the Himalayas. I lived in a cave above Gangotri from where the holy Ganga begins its course.' She observed the strictest vow of silence and lived off whatever wild berries were available at that height (21,000 feet), sucking icicles to slake her thirst.

Apparently, she was back in the plains in the early 1940s—and politically active. There was a warrant for her arrest during the 1942 Quit India Movement. She evaded it by remaining underground. She was taken very ill and for a while was treated by sadhus in the jungles of Koil Ghati.

It was early in 1943 that she decided to be formally initiated into a sanyasi order. As required by tradition, she first sought the permission of her adoptive mother. By now Mateshwari, as she called her, had reconciled herself to her daughter's waywardness and gave her consent. At Ayodhya she was accepted as a dandiswami sanyasin by Sri Karpatriji. She was given yet another name, Sushriyananda Saraswati—a name no one used. Before the initiation there was considerable debate on the issue as neither a woman nor anyone who was not a Brahmin had been admitted by the Sankarapeeth. The Arya Samaj supported her against the orthodox elements. For some time after the initiation ceremony she stayed in the village temple built by her mother. Then suddenly one morning, clad in her deer skin and with kamandal in her hand, she disappeared from her village to return to her cave in the Himalayan vastness.

KALI REINCARNATED

How and when she returned to civilization is shrouded in mystery. According to her sometime in the year 1946 she found herself in the Kali Temple in Calcutta. The 'transport' had been preceded by a mystic experience during Navratri when she had a clear vision of the Kali enthroned in Kalighat. It was accompanied by ecstatic vibrations ('spirit of pure joy' is how she describes it) and a subtle emanation of fragrance of sandalwood. She felt that the goddess had sent for her to make her an instrument of some divine design. She describes the mystic journey, analogous to the holy Ganga's descent from Gangotri to the Bay of Bengal. She spent the day amongst the throng of worshippers. Apparently her presence did not attract any attention. When the evening service was over, she hid herself behind the goddess. The priests locked the sanctum without noticing her. She spent the night in prayer and meditation. Next morning, when the head priest, Haripada Bandopadhyaya, opened the temple door, he saw standing beside the statue of the goddess a young woman who looked every inch a fair reincarnation of Kali: long tresses falling down to her shoulder, torso covered with leopard skin, trident in one hand, kamandal in the other. He prostrated himself before her.

The news spread like wildfire through the metropolis. Pilgrims in their thousands came to pay her homage. Offerings of fruit, flowers, coconuts, silver and gold jewellery were heaped at her feet. Amongst her visitors was Justice Rama Prasad Mukherjee of the High Court of Calcutta who was the elder brother of Shyama Prasad Mukherjee, minister in Nehru's cabinet.

Shraddha Mata was persuaded to give up her vow of silence to give her message to the people. For several weeks following she was housed in the palace of Rani Rasmoni in Dakshineshwar (where before her Swami Vivekananda and Sister Nivedita had stayed). She was invited to expound on the Gita. She did so to large audiences, sometimes addressing four meetings in a day. But she never failed to spend some time of the day or night at the Kali Temple. Her chief achievement was to persuade the priests and worshippers to give up sacrificing animals to the goddess and instead make offerings of corn, grain and vegetables.

THE NEHRU CONNECTION

Shraddha Mata was not very anxious to discuss her relationship with Nehru; I did not press her on the subject. But, in the course of our dialogue, Mathai's insinuations in his two books on Nehru and the conjectures made by the press surfaced. In several interviews given to a variety of journals, she has said that it was Shyama Prasad Mukherjee who brought her to Delhi and fixed the interview with the Prime Minister. She was given fifteen minutes to have her say; she was with him for an hour and a half. What she said to Nehru in the first meeting can be briefly summed up as follows: Nehru's secularism ignored the religious and cultural traditions of India and had therefore little support of the sadhus and sanyasis who were guardians of these traditions. Nehru did not give Sanskrit the place it deserved as the mother of all languages. He had toyed with the idea of introducing the Roman script to replace Devanagari and other vernacular scripts. He wanted the wording in the Constitution to be 'India that is Bharat' instead of what it finally emerged under her insistence as 'Bharat that is India'. And so on.

I told her that I had gathered from some members of Nehru's household that she had met Nehru no more than three or four times. She smiled and replied: 'That's all they know about. I will tell you what I have not told anyone before. At the very first meeting that took place in the house on Aurangzeb Road we established a rapport which seemed to indicate that we had known each other in our previous lives. I could see Panditji was attracted to me. He was impressed with what I had to say. And I do not deny that he was attracted towards this,' she said pointing to her face and features. 'I met him many times and for many hours at a stretch. I sensed his growing attachment to me. He asked me many times about my marriage and my husband. I can say that had I been free and not taken the vows of a sanyasin, it would have been me and not any of the other women whose names have been linked with him (Lady Edwina Mountbatten, Padmaja Naidu, Mridula Sarabhai) that he would have wanted to marry. But it never came to it. I told him quite firmly that I was a sanyasin and that he as a Brahmin was expected to honour Hindu tradition. At one time he addressed me in his letter as Priya rather than Mata as others did, and I told him that was not proper. He did not repeat it.' With some hesitation I asked her if the relationship, as stated by Mathai, had gone beyond the platonic. She replied in two words spoken with considerable feeling: 'Asat hai (It is not true).'

Like other relationships, the Nehru-Shraddha Mata association became the victim of misunderstandings—some of them deliberately planted in Nehru's mind by people like Mathai—whom she describes as a member of the anti-Hindu lobby. There is little doubt that Shraddha Mata spoke the language of Hindu obscurantists like that of the leaders of the RSS. She admits that at one time Nehru told her that she saw everything from the Hindu point of view. The meetings became less frequent and then ceased altogether.

For a while Shraddha Mata lived in the Harijan basti in Delhi, then at the invitation of Raja Jugal Kishore Birla, she moved to Birla House, then to Birla Mandir and finally to a hut constructed for her on the ridge behind the temple. She was in Faridabad the day Gandhiji was assassinated. She spent the following fortnight chanting hymns from the Gita.

Sometime in 1952, Shraddha went abroad. She toured Europe, the United States, East Africa—and everywhere she went she gave discourses on the Gita, which were heard by large crowds. When she returned to India she did not bother to contact Nehru. The Maharaja of Jaipur, Sawai Man Singh and his wife, the luscious Gayatri Devi, had become her disciples. He gifted the Hathroi Fort to Shraddha Mata. She moved to Jaipur and she set up her 'world peace army'. Panditji misunderstood her intentions and regarded her venture as an attempt to revive feudal traditions among erstwhile Rajput princes. 'Sukhadia created mischief,' she says (M. L. Sukhadia was then chief minister of Rajasthan). 'When Nehru visited Jaipur, a mehfil was arranged by Hari Bhan Upadhyaya. I was cordial. But distant.' When Nehru had his first stroke, Shraddha Mata wrote to him expressing her concern. He replied asking her to forget her past bitterness. That was the last communication between them. 'When I was close to him I could transmit some of my shakti to him,' she says. 'Once distance had been created, I was no longer able to do so. I could not help him in his affliction.'

Her reference to Panditji's death gave me the opportunity to ask her what she made of death and dying. Her views are traditionally Hindu. According to her, one lot of human beings evolve from human birth to human rebirth, getting closer and closer to the light eternal. The other lot who have evil within them go through all eighty-four lakh yonis till they are purged of their evil. I protested. 'Mataji, you are only making statements; there is no evidence to substantiate any of this eighty-four lakh yoni business.' She replied in excellent English: 'There can be no empirical evidence for this kind of thing. You can only realize the truth through insight brought about during samadhi. No one can provide physical proof of such phenomena because cosmic truth is reflected when man goes beyond sensory perceptions.' I asked her to explain why if there was a God there was so much injustice in the world? Why good men suffered and evil men prospered? Once again she explained in the traditional 'Pichley janmon key karm (Paying for deeds done in past lives).' All this was beyond me. So was her reasoning about why there ought to be nine Durga Pujas and not eight or ten. 'Because,' she maintained, 'ultimately energy is in nine stages of radiation, one layer after the other—that is the tantric belief.'

The next morning I was made more aware of the great gulf that divides the agnostic from the believer. We were seated on the parapet of the fort. It was very warm. A cord connecting the table fan to the switch came loose. Surendra Singh who had just come down from the temple after a session of prayer and meditation plugged it back in. Then he pointed to a naked patch on the cord and said, 'You see, by mistake I touched the naked wire but it did not give me any shock! That is because the shakti generated by prayer and meditation is still in me.' Shraddha Mata endorsed this by adding: 'And also because I am here beside you.' I was sorely tempted to ask Surendra Singh to touch the live wire again and let me see the power of spiritual shakti pitted against the electrical, but I did not want to be thrown out.

MATHAI: HE IS A LIAR

I had planned to put off the questions about her association with Pandit Nehru to the last so that I could get the rest of her life story before running the risk of an abrupt dismissal. But she had brought up the subject herself so many times that I was sure she would not be upset by my asking her for further elucidation. 'Mathai in his first book has written that after returning from Bangalore you had settled in Jaipur as a mod young lady with short-cropped hair, using lipstick and wearing jeans... Is that so?'

Shraddha Mata exploded in a string of expletives: 'Ullu ka pattha! Moorakh! Agyani! His skull needs examining. See all these letters.' She unwrapped a bundle of letters and handed me one from the late Sawai Man Singh, Maharaja of Jaipur, donating Hathroi Fort to her. It began 'Respected Mataji' and ended with 'yours devoted S. Man Singh'. Shraddha Mata asked me: 'You think the Maharaja would have addressed me in this way and given me property worth over two crore rupees if I was wearing lipstick and slacks?'

(1979)

MATAJI AND THE HIPPIES

An act of betrayal drove her to the banks at the Ganga. Old and ugly now, she takes under her wing six lost souls seeking the light. Preaching, praying, feeding and smoking ganja, she holds court in a boat. But history repeats itself in strange ways...

She sat on her haunches with nothing more than a saffron dhoti covering her body. She rubbed ganja in the palm of her hand. She was stocky as a filled-up gunnysack. Beads of sweat rolling off her body... age on her face...a trident tattooed on her forehead. A double-decker bun of matted hair atop.

She intoned the name of Shiv Shankar and gave me her blessing. Sitting with her were her disciples—five young men and a girl. They were Americans who had wandered around the world in search of peace of mind and had ultimately found it in Benares in Mataji's little houseboat tethered on the banks of the holy Ganga. I took my seat beside her.

Mataji rammed ganja down the nozzle of her long chillum. She wrapped a wet rag round the stem, put it reverently against her forehead and roared the invocation of her patron deity:

Bhum bhum bhum bhum Alakh Niranjan. God of the Burning Ghats. Destroyer of Sorrows.

The girl who wore a purple sarong around her waist got up. She made a taper from a piece of newspaper and lit it from an oil lamp burning in the corner. Mataji put the chillum to her lips as if she were blowing a sacred conch. The girl put the flaming taper to the pipe, Mataji inhaled deeply till the ganja was aflame. She took five quick puffs and then held her breath. She shut her eyes and held her breath; the veins of her neck seemed to be bursting. She handed the chillum to the girl; her eyes were bloodshot. The girl bowed, took the chillum and, like Mataji, pressed it against her forehead before smoking it. She passed it on to her fellow disciples.

The houseboat was tethered at some distance from the ghat used as a cremation ground. I noticed that the inside of the boat was clean and tidy. On the wall there were many nude figurines dyed in deep colours. On a string nailed to the two sides were hung trousers, bush shirts and dhotis of many garish colours—green and pink and yellow. There were also a few loincloths. The disciples sat in silence while Mataji jabbered away at the top of her voice. Her speech was punctuated with loud slogans in honour of her gods. They imbibed every word she said as if it was nectar.

Beside her was sprawled a young man in shorts with whiskers like those of Genghis Khan. Next to him was a blue-eyed boy; then a youngster with a massive butcher's beard. The fourth wore sadhu's earrings and a saffron-coloured loincloth.

The fifth sat rigidly in the lotus pose. On his yellow dhoti was printed 'Ram Ram'. He was so thin and woebegone that each time he inhaled ganja he burst into violent coughs and his head collapsed on his navel. The girl was blonde, her hair tumbled over her shoulders down to her purple dhoti. She too wore the mark of the trident on her forehead; her eyelids had a green shadow about them. On her arms she wore several bracelets of basil seeds.

Mataji was saying, 'I've to bathe them, feed them, teach them. I give them a hundred sermons. If I did not look after these poor creatures they would die of hunger. They're lost souls; they have dirty ways. You would not believe it but they eat with the same hand with which they wipe their bottoms.' Her eyes sparkled when she emphasized her horror of their doings.

She nodded towards the chap with the butcher's beard. 'He's my Rama. Those two seated across are Bharata and Lakshmana and that chap sprawled at my feet is Kumbhakarna; and this girl is my favourite, Nandini. In her last life she was a fish in the Ganga. She performed good deeds and has been given human rebirth. And that fellow sitting across there in padmasana is my Prem Das. He does not eat or drink. Nothing stays in his stomach.' She paused and said, 'I must now go and make arrangements for their food. All they can do is to sit like cats staring at me.' She got up and quickly swept out of the houseboat.

The young man in the saffron loincloth began to read loudly from a book on Confucius. The butcher-bearded Rama took out his flute and softly intoned the notes of the Raaga Bhairavi. The famished Prem Das sitting in the lotus pose engaged me in conversation. 'We do not take ganja for its intoxicant effect or as a drink. This is worship. We are seeking ourselves. Who are we? Why? Where are we bound for? The past is dead, the future is lost. The older generation has sold our birthright. We have to atone for their follies. This 'now' is helpless... We... We are disillusioned and blinded. We cannot see objects lying under our very noses.' He lit a cigarette and blew two jets of smoke through his nostrils. He continued, 'Can you see any images in these jets of smoke? Can you see that the entire world is contained in the burning up of this cigarette? In this I see volcanoes erupting. I see valleys flooded with molten lava—cities reduced to ashes.' He continued to smoke with his eyes fixed on the burning end of his cigarette. I asked: 'Have you ever tried LSD?'

'Three times. Each time I saw new worlds open up before me. But in order to take LSD you have to be in the proper frame of mind. You must have a guru, or someone who has been on the trip before. Here, it is only the Mataji who can do so.'

We began to discuss Mataji's philosophy of salvation. There are many things said about Mataji on the banks of the Ganga. Some said that she had an affair with her cook. They had both come on a pilgrimage and the cook was swept away by the stream. Mataji had refused to return to her home.

Others said that a party of sadhus had found her as an abandoned child in a bear's cave and they had brought her to the Kumbh Mela and in time left her to the mercies of the holy river. Yet others said that she was descended from the Rani of Jhansi and had been performing penance and practising austerity for several incarnations.

Prem Das had yet another version. 'Mataji is from Gwalior. Her old father ran a paan-bidi shop on the main road. Different kinds of people came to this shop—truck drivers, tradesmen, tourists and sometimes gangs of dacoits. Mataji spent the day folding paan leaves for her customers. She was then eighteen, beautiful and bursting with youthfulness. She fell in love with a young Rajput named Mangal Singh.

'Mangal Singh was the son of a wealthy landowner. He became a regular visitor to her father's shop. It is there that he got to know that gangs of dacoits were in the habit of visiting the shop and drinking. One day Mangal Singh tricked the dacoits, informed the police and had them arrested. He had done all this because of his love for the eighteen-year-old girl. But the act of betrayal only converted Mataji's love into hatred. Mangal Singh tried hundreds of ways to ask her forgiveness, but Mataji would not relent. "Get out of my sight, you are a low-born cur. Anyone who had suckled at the breasts of a Rajput mother would not practise such treachery. I do not want to see your face for the rest of my life."

'Mataji was so upset by this incident that she left her home one night and for many years she went about with parties of sadhus and then ended up here on the banks of the Ganga.'

Prem Das spoke to me for almost two hours. I promised to see him again the next day and returned to my hotel. Many days later when I had nothing particular to do I decided to call on Mataji again. I bought a dozen bananas and apples and went to the houseboat. As I approached the houseboat I saw her striding up and down the sand bank. As soon as she saw me a broad smile lit her face. She greeted me: 'Alakh Niranjan. Come along, Son. The God of the Burning Ghats sent you here.' She took me into the houseboat. Her disciples were sprawled on the floor. Only Prem Das was as usual sitting in the lotus pose with his eyes fixed on a spot on the wall. His ribs showed through his chest. Mataji said: 'Shankar has brought some fruits for you, get up. You've not eaten anything since yesterday.'

She sat down and crossed her legs. I placed the basket of fruits before her. She picked up a banana exactly as it were her chillum, pressed it against her forehead, intoned the name of her gods, broke the fruit into two and threw away half as an offering to the sacred Ganga. The other half she gave to the butcher-bearded boy. He, too, pressed it against his forehead before he ate it. Mataji did not eat any of the fruit. She peeled and cut the bananas and apples and fed her brood. Only Prem Das did not eat.

Mataji said: 'My Prem Das will eat nothing today because I am fasting. It is masya—moonless night. Victory to Darkness! Victory to the God of the Burning Ghats!'

I asked Mataji, 'You make no secret of smoking ganja—what if the police found out?'

She replied: 'Ganja is a herb sacred to Lord Shiva. It's no crime to smoke it. In Benares alone there are eleven licensed ganja vendors. No one dare interfere with my sacred ritual. The Lord of the Burning Ghats would surely reduce him to cinders.' To emphasize the point she stuck the sharp end of her trident into the wooden floor of the boat. With her red ganja-besotted eyes she glowered at me and cried, 'Alakh Niranjan.' One banana and apple each made the disciples hungrier. Kumbhakarna pleaded, 'Mataji, please go to the bazaar and get us something to eat.'

'When it's time, I'll go,' she replied. 'I haven't yet received the Divine Command.'

The disciples were silenced. At last Mataji relented. She rose and said, 'All right. I'll go and get you people something to eat. And for you, Prem Das, rice and yoghurt.' She hurried out of the boat.

The group maintained its silence for a while. Then Kumbhakarna spoke. 'Sometimes the spirit of Chandi, the Goddess of Destruction, comes into the body of our Mataji. When she loses her temper, we do not take it ill.'

Suddenly there was a commotion outside. Shouting, stamping of heavy hobnailed boots. The boat rocked. A huge police officer burst in. He had a pistol in his hand. A posse of armed constables followed him. The disciples sat where they were, lost in the maze of ganja fumes, unconcerned. I panicked. The police officer bared a row of glistening white dentures; his walrus moustache dyed a glossy black gave him a ghoulish appearance. 'Stay where you are!' he growled, pointing his weapon at the group.

The constables began to look through the disciples' bags, passports and papers. Their visas had expired. The officer ordered them out of the boat. The constables gathered their ganja chillums.

The officer noticed me. He sniffed near my mouth to see if I had ganja odour. He asked my name and occupation and asked me to stand aside.

'Take the lot to the station,' he ordered.

The disciples submitted without a protest. They were like a bunch of passive resisters. Their faces glowed with beatific resignation. Only

Prem Das murmured: 'I am not well. You will have to feed me rice and yoghurt.'

The police officer ignored the request. 'March the bloody lot to the station,' he barked.

Down the sandbank came Mataji. Her arms were loaded with provisions. The setting sun lit her ash-and-sweat-smeared body in a crimson glow. She saw the police party and roared like a wounded tigress: 'How dare you interrupt the worship of Bhairava! Get the hell out of here or the Lord of the Burning Ghats will reduce you to cinders!' She descended like a thunderbolt.

'Get hold of the bitch,' screamed the police officer.

Mataji strode down till she came face to face with the officer. Her face was like a sheet of red hot iron. For a moment time came to a petrified standstill. The constables, the disciples and I gaped spellbound at the confrontation. They glowered at each other. Sparks flew. The trident on Mataji's forehead shone. Her eyes were like volcano craters.

The officer's eyes gradually lost their fire. His gaze shifted from Mataji's face to the setting sun. He stepped back, put his pistol back in its holster and said to his men, 'Release them.'

Mataji walked triumphantly back into her boat. We collected our belongings and followed her. The exhibition of her divine power had us completely spellbound.

Mataji fed us. The sun went down. The dusky soot of twilight mingled in the waters of the Ganga. I asked permission to leave. Mataji replied: 'It is masya—the moonless night meant for prayer. Stay and join us.'

Mataji took out new earthenware oil lamps and dipped them in the stream. She filled them with coconut oil, rolled wicks, lit them and put them around the image of Shiva. She went out and bathed in the Ganga and came back to us. She was wearing a fresh sari bordered with red and had let down her long hair. She chanted at the top of her voice, 'Bhum...Bhum...Bhum.' Her disciples took up the chant. Mataji said, 'You go on with the worship. I must go and pay my homage to the Lord of the Burning Ghats. I'll be back soon.' The worship continued. The smoke from the lamps and the fumes of ganja filled the boat with acrid vapours.

We waited till midnight. There was no sign of Mataji. Then we heard footsteps come up the gangway. A man stood at the door. We could not see him clearly, only his white muslin shirt and dhoti flapped in the breeze. He came in. He was big and his walrus moustache hung down to his chin. Prem Das asked: 'Have you come to see Mataji?'

'Yes,' replied the man. 'Forgive me for disturbing you at this hour. Where is she?'

Prem Das growled at the man and said, 'Haven't I seen you somewhere before?'

The stranger smiled and replied: 'Earlier in the day I was the Superintendent of Police, now I've come here as just Mangal Singh.'

Prem Das and I exchanged glances. Prem Das asked Mangal Singh to sit down and said: 'Mataji has been away since eight o'clock. She said she was going to pay homage to the Lord of the Burning Ghats and would be back soon.'

Mangal Singh appeared startled. A shadow crossed his face and he shook his head and said: 'She will never come back again.'

(1969)

DAYANAND SARASWATI: PROFILE OF A RENAISSANCE CRUSADER

The secret of the phenomenal success as a reformer of Swami Dayanand, whose ninety-seventh death anniversary falls next week on 30 October, lay in the fact that he stuck fast to traditional Hindu rituals (agyopavit, shradhs and havan), observed Hindu traditions and made the Vedas the sole repositories of the truth, both religious and scientific.

Thus solidly entrenched in Hinduism he was able to launch frontal attacks on idol worship which he regarded as un-Hindu and to condemn practices like discrimination against lower castes and castigation of widows as harmful to Hindu society.

By glorifying the past of Aryavarta and denouncing the degradation of Hindu society under alien rule, he fanned the dying embers of Hindu self-respect into flames of Hindu nationalism. Arya Samaj leaders, like the late Lala Lajpat Rai, who were at the forefront of the freedom movement and a large majority of terrorists from northern India, including Sardar Bhagat Singh, were influenced by the Arya Samaj.

Echoes of Dayanand's teachings can be heard today in the pronouncements of the leaders of the Bharatiya Janata Party and the RSS.

Dayanand was by all accounts a most remarkable man. Not much is known about his childhood because he rarely spoke about his parents and his family. And by the time he had become famous most of his relatives and childhood companions were dead or untraceable. He was born in Tankara, a small town in the Morvi state of Kathiawar, the eldest of five children of a devoutly religious Samvedi Audichya Shaivite Brahmin who was also a man of wealth—a landowner, tax collector and moneylender. The exact date of Dayanand's birth is not known. But we know that his pre-sanyasi name was Dayaram Mulshankar Tiwari and he was generally known as Mulji.

The family were strict in the observance of ritual, particularly the evening prayer, Sandhya. It was during Shivratri when he saw mice clambering over the Shivalinga and nibbling at the offerings that Mulji became very critical of idol worship. The deaths of his nineteen-year-old sister and an uncle who was his mentor, and to whom he was deeply attached, made a deep impression on his mind over the transitoriness of life. The pressure of his parents wanting him to marry drove him from home, and to abandon grihastha and take to sanyas. When he took the vagrant oath of the ascetic he was barely twenty-one years old.

The impact of the years in his parents' home and the religious atmosphere in Kathiawar were to remain with him all his life: the obsession with Shaivite ritual and the emphasis on Sanskrit he imbibed from his parents. The air he breathed was heavy with Vaishnavism and Jainism. As a Shaivite Brahmin he learnt to disapprove of both, and found Adi Shankaracharya's unqualified monism more suited to his philosophic bent of mind.

Nevertheless, Mulji was first initiated into a Vaishnav order and took on the name Shuddha Chaitanya. This did not last long. His father brought him back home and tried once more to force him to marry. Once more Mulji fled his home and this time entered the Shaivite ashram at Chetan Math. It was here that he went over to the Vedantic concept of the oneness of God and man—Aham Brahma Asmi; here on the banks of the Narmada he was initiated into the Sanyasi order of Dandis (one of the Dashanami Sadhu sects) and given a name which he was destined to make famous: Dayanand Saraswati.

WANDERING MONK

Dayanand travelled northwards to Mount Abu and eastwards to Haridwar to attend the Kumbh Mela in December 1854 and again the greater Kumbh in 1855. He spent the rest of the year in the Himalayas where he came into contact with the tantrics. He studied the Tantra Shastras, tried out Hatha Yoga and even imbibed hashish. He records that at Garhmukteshwar he hauled a corpse out of the river and cut it up with a knife to see for himself whether what the Tantra Shastras said about human biology was in fact true.

He wrote: 'I came to the firm conclusion that there was not the slightest similarity between the texts and the corpse. I then tore the books to pieces and threw them into the river with the remains of the corpse.'

After four years of wandering (of which we know little except that he visited Kanpur, Allahabad, Varanasi and other cities of UP) Dayanand arrived at Mathura in 1860 and became a disciple of the famous Sanskrit grammarian, the blind Swami Virajananda (1779-1868). He was now thirty-six years old. It was the blind Guru who opened Dayanand's eyes to the need of reviving pristine Hinduism and the ideal of Karma Yoga—the path of action. Instead of receiving the farewell dakshina, the Guru extracted a promise from his disciple 'to devote everything, even give up your life, to the propagation in India of the books of the rishis and the Vedic religion.'

Mathura, the centre of the Krishna cult in its most decadent form, changed Dayanand from a simple scholar of Sanskrit and the Vedas into a preacher. By now he had picked up enough Hindi to be able to partake in debate. He began to tour other cities: Agra, Gwalior, Karauli, Jaipur, Ajmer, Pushkar. The only weapons in Dayanand's armoury were the Vedas. But these he used to devastate all opposition.

GOD IS NIRANKAR

The Vedas, he maintained, propagated strict monotheism. God was Nirankar (unmanifested) Paramatma and was the only phenomenon which was at once truth, consciousness and bliss: Satchidananda. And those who believed in the Puranas and worshipped idols had strayed from the path of true Hinduism. The Bhagvata Purana, he declared, was totally spurious. 'Abandon the application of ashes, abandon the wearing of the rudraksh, and do not adore the Lord of Universe in the form of a Shivalinga.'

It took a little longer for Dayanand to reject the caste system—but eventually he did that too. On the positive side, he advocated the Sandhya ritual, the recitation of the Gayatri Mantra and the practice of Hatha Yoga—but only for physical well-being.

The next time Swamiji went to Kumbh at Haridwar, he went flaunting the saffron flag with the motto 'Pakhand Khandini' denouncing the very concept of purification through bathing in holy water. 'This is only water,' he said, referring to the Ganga. 'Moksha does not come from water, it comes from works.'

Here was a Brahmin ascetic, clad in a loincloth, carrying a staff and begging bowl, denouncing all that traditional Brahminism stood for. He wandered around the cities and villages of Uttar Pradesh, sleeping on the ground with a stone for his pillow. When not addressing people, he studied other religions and the English language. As the Muslims claimed the Quran to be the word of God, so did Dayanand claim divinity for the Vedas. It is to the Vedas he turned to denounce astrology as deceit and the Bhrigu Samhita as fraud.

Swami Dayanand was convinced that it was only through knowledge of Sanskrit and the Vedas that Hinduism as it was practised in ancient Aryavarta could be revived. He started with a Sanskrit school at Farrukhabad. At the time Farrukhabad had a small puritanical community: the Sadhus, who believed in the teachings of Kabir and Nanak, were monotheists and against idol worship and caste distinctions. Swamiji, though he disapproved of the Sadhus as deviants from purely Vedantic Hinduism, probably felt that the learning of Sanskrit and the Vedas would put this otherwise good set of people back on the right path.

Dayanand's direct exposure to Christianity and its impact on Hinduism came when he visited Calcutta in December 1872. He was welcomed by the leaders of the Brahmo Samaj: Keshab Chandra Sen, Rajnarayan Bose, the scholar of divinity, Ishwar Chandra Vidyasagar and the historian R. C. Dutt. The Brahmos persuaded him to start wearing clothes and to pay more attention to Christianity and Islam than he had done hitherto. He not only changed his lifestyle (on his visit to Aligarh he entered the city riding on an elephant) but also greatly widened his horizons. It was after his visit to Calcutta that he spelt out his ideas in his first edition of *Satyarth Prakash* published in 1875.

THE DOCTRINE

In the *Satyarth Prakash* Swamiji reaffirmed his conviction in the unique divinity of the Vedas. He also wrote that while the Vedas were of universal application to all mankind, the Bible and the Quran were only meant for followers of Christianity and Islam. Swamiji painted a very rosy picture of Aryavarta, the Golden Age of Hinduism, and elevated Sanskrit as the mother language, of all languages which he denigrated as later corruptions.

Apart from theological affirmations about the nature of the godhead, Swamiji maintained that the basis of scientific discoveries including steam-powered engines, hydroelectric energy, the telegraph and even atomic energy were to be found in the Vedas.

Swami Dayanand's fervent belief in his brand of Hinduism left no room for other religious systems like Christianity and Islam, which he regarded as foreign importations. He also refused to accept variations of Hinduism like the teachings of Vallabhacharya or the pronouncements of Bhaktas like Kabir and Nanak. Even the Brahmos, whom he had initially admired, he later criticized for their love of the English and their anglicized way of living.

The *Satyarth Prakash* dealt with other subjects like marriage, caste, diet, administration and politics. After giving credit to the British for introducing the rule of law, he criticized the way the courts functioned in India. He advocated the abolition of the tax on salt and heavier excise on liquor.

Having propounded his views in print, Swamiji decided to set up an organization which would ensure their propagation for posterity. During his stay in Bombay he founded the Arya Samaj on 10 April 1875. Maharashtra leaders including M. C. Ranade and Mahatma Phule lent their support to the Samaj. The nucleus of the Bombay branch consisted largely of the trading banias and Maharashtrian Brahmins.

Swami Dayanand spent the following year touring UP and made his first visit to Delhi in 1877. That spring he engaged himself in debates with leaders of the Muslims and Christians. By this time Swamiji had been acknowledged as the greatest, albeit controversial, leader of renascent Hinduism. When he proceeded northwards from Delhi he was welcomed by Punjab's Hindus and Sikhs (who had obviously not yet read the *Satyarth)*. The sixteen months he spent in the Punjab were in some ways his most successful as well as his most disastrous in shaping the future of Hindu-Sikh relations. While large numbers of Hindu Khatris and Aroras turned to him eagerly, the Sikhs turned sour against him and his followers. His movement to convert (shuddhi) Muslims and Christians raised the ire of Christian missionaries and Muslim mullahs. Consequently, while the Arya Samaj found an enthusiastic following amongst educated, urban Hindus, it earned the hostility of Muslims, Christians and Sikhs.

Swamiji never returned to the Punjab but it was in the Punjab (and present day Haryana) that his teaching took firmer root than in UP, Rajasthan or Maharashtra where he toured extensively (opening new branches of the Samaj wherever he went).

The strain of continuous travel, addressing meetings and entering into debates began to tell on Swamiji's health. One illness followed another. In 1880 he drew up his first will. But neither illness nor premonition of death made any difference to his schedule of lectures and debates. It was not all triumphal processions: debates often turned acrimonious and sometime even led to the exchange of legal notices.

Swamiji's brief encounter with the Theosophists was not fruitful. To start with they were attracted by the Arya Samaj and even suggested making a kind of united organization to be called the Theosophical Society. They later accused him of ambition to become the messiah of a new faith. Swamiji denied this: 'I do not wish to found a new religion. I only preach the eternal Vedic faith. I do not aspire to any position except that of a preacher,' he wrote to Madame Blavatsky and denounced Theosophy as humbug.

AMONG PRINCES

Swami Dayanand aspired to bring the masses of Hindus to his way of thinking through conversions of the princely order: yatha raja, tatha praja—as the ruler, so the ruled. The Rajasthan branch of the Samaj had the Maharana of Udaipur as president and included the rulers of Shalipura, Asind and Masuda on its council. Swamiji performed yagnas, blessed princes on their ascension to their gaddis, and exhorted them to be monogamous, give up drink and pursuit of pleasure.

His note of admonition to Raja Jaswant Singh of Jodhpur is an example of his outspokenness: 'It is such a great pity that, though you are such an intelligent man, you still keep engaging, I do not know why, in the following activities: drinking, consorting with prostitutes, kite-flying, gambling. If you do not give up those pastimes and devote at least six hours a day to state affairs, and if you do not show greater affection for your wives, princesses of great beauty, it is a great pity indeed. As a ruler is, so will the people be. All these bad habits are extremely injurious to your life expectation, your strength and health, your fame to the achievement of the aims of dharma, artha, kama, and moksha, and to the parental care for your subjects: On the love of husband and wife depends the welfare of the whole family: its absence destroys the whole line. Therefore, do not waste your precious time in drinking, womanizing, etc., but spend it in the good work of looking after your subjects according to the sacred law of justice, and thus become worthy of universal fame and gratitude.'

Swamiji was taken ill in September and removed to Mount Abu and then to Ajmer where he died on 30 October 1883. It was later rumoured (he had earlier given currency to the rumour) that he had been administered poison at the behest of the Jodhpur Rana's mistress, Nanni. There is little evidence available on the subject. More significant were his views on how he wished to be commemorated. 'Throw the ashes of my body somewhere in a field, thus they will be of some use; but do not make a memorial, lest that be the start of some idolatry.'

SAMAJ SPILT

Two years after the death of Swami Dayanand, the Arya Samaj split into two. The progressives, led by Lala Lajpat Rai, believed that Swamiji stood for modern education, freedom to eat whatever anyone liked, saving the cow and the universality of their creed. The conservatives opted for the ancient, Sanskrit-based education of the gurukulas, vegetarianism and the Samaj's teaching being restricted to the Hindu-born. Nevertheless, between the two they set up an impressive number of DAV schools, colleges, orphanages and gurukulas, young men's and women's Arya associations, Vedic salvation army, Arya publishing houses financed by a 1 per cent voluntary tax on the income of members. In due course, the Arya Samaj became the most powerful social and religious political force in northern India stretching far beyond the Indus in the north to eastern Uttar Pradesh. It also had a considerable following in Rajasthan, Madhya Pradesh, Gujarat and Maharashtra.

Swami Dayanand's role as the regenerator of Hinduism should be viewed in its historical perspective of a Hindu India humbled, ruled, exploited and reviled for centuries by Muslim and European conquerors. What the Muslims thought of the Hindus was aptly summed up by Al-Biruni. 'They sip the urine of cows, they use turbans as trousers, they spit and blow their noses without respect for those present.'

Even a liberal intellectual like Aldous Huxley described India as 'depressing as no other country I have ever known. One breathes in it not air, but dust and hopelessness.' It was this kind of gloomy vision of India that reformers had to dispel by restoring among the masses confidence in their Hindu heritage.

Of them Dayanand was the first and the foremost. While Raja Ram Mohan Roy turned to the Upanishads (and Swami Vivekananda to Vedanta), Dayanand went back to the principal source of Hinduism, the Vedas, which he lauded as 'eternal, infallible and the only revelation of truth given by God to men'. For him and his followers Judaism, Christianity and Islam were garbled versions of Vedic teachings. He believed that India was the cradle of all cultures, Sanskrit the mother of all languages, Vedic knowledge the basis of all scientific discovery including radio, radar, television, atomic bombs and all advances in medicine.

STRIDE FORWARD

This may sound somewhat fatuous and should be taken with a massive dose of salt, but there is little doubt that in the realm of theology Dayanand cleared many cobwebs from the minds of the Hindus. He explained the multiplicity of gods in the Rig Veda which mentioned thirty-three manifestations of the One God; lit the spark of karma in a community which had resigned itself to passive acceptance of everything that happened; and he explained away miracle-loaded sagas of the Mahabharata and the Ramayana as fairy tales. His insistence on monogamy, condemnation of Sati, child marriages, purdah and allowing widows the right to sit through niyoga marks a giant stride forward to freedom from superstition and unwholesome social customs. He drove idols and priests out of his temples and threw them open to all who were willing to purify themselves through shuddhi.

Dayanand's Arya Samaj was like a double-edged sword. While its one side clove through the dead wood of decadent ritualism and made Hindus forward-looking, proud of their heritage and fiercely nationalistic, the other side cut asunder the tenuous bonds that Hindu society had developed with other religious communities—the Muslims, Christians, Jains and Sikhs. It will not be stretching one's imagination too much to question if Dayanand would not have (were he alive today) propagated the ideal of an Akhand Bharat, a Hindi (Sanskrit)-Hindu-Hindustan, supported the RSS and the Jan Sangh, sought to bring Jains and Sikhs back into the Hindu fold, agitated for the expulsion of Christian missionaries, and asked the Muslims of India who had supported the demand for Pakistan to leave for Pakistan.

For all his learning, Dayanand did not have much respect for views at variance with his own. He would have had little patience with the ideal 'sarva dharma sambhava (respect for all religions)' of Mahatma Gandhi and even less for the near-agnostic secularism of Pandit Nehru.

(1980)

MEMORIES OF BHAI VIR SINGH

The last time I met Bhai Vir Singh was three months ago in Amritsar. He was a sick man under the care of nurses and doctors. His bed and sitting rooms were heated by Canadian stoves and a constant watch was kept on the temperature. The doctor had forbidden him to work or receive visitors. There were only a few exceptions to this rule; amongst them were younger writers for whom Vir Singh always had a sort of personal regard. He walked into the sitting room slowly but unescorted. I touched his feet; he put his frail hand on my shoulder and asked me to sit down beside him. He enquired about my children for he always loved children. He spoke with effort and had to pause for breath after each sentence and then became silent. He was never a man of too many words and the custom of the circle around him was to sit in silence and meditate. After ten minutes he looked up and smiled. I knew I was expected to leave.

'When will you be going to the hills?' I asked.

He raised one hand in a gesture of resignation and answered: 'Who knows!'

LONGING FOR TOUCH

I got up and once more touched his feet. This time he took my hands in his—his soft, warm hands which had the ability to stir deep emotions and without rhyme or reason bring tears to one's eyes.

'Give my love to your daughter. God bless you.'

I hurried out of the room. It was obvious that his time was fast running out. He did not seem concerned because to him life had meant reading and writing and the doctor had forbidden him both. And he was of the philosophical mould, those who take both life and death in their stride. I left his house but the memory of his touch lingered for a long time. Therein lay the secret of one of the dominant themes in his poems—a sensuous longing for physical contact with God in the tradition of the Vaishnava and Sufi writers, a sort of mystic belief that the touch would evoke the angelic in man and, as a philosopher's stone, transmute dross to gold.

> You struck the chords
> And I burst into music
> Like a harp attuned.
> You forsook me
> And I feel silent
> As one stricken dumb.
> Thy hand hath the magic touch.
> It makes the living come to Life.

The 'touch' had mystical significance for Vir Singh. It occurs often in his writing:

> In a dream You came to me
> I leapt to hold You in my embrace;
> It was but a fantasy I could not hold
> And my arms ached with longing.
> Then I rushed to clasp Your feet
> To lay my head thereon:
> Even these I could not reach
> For You were high and I was low.

TWENTY YEARS AFTER

This last meeting was a strange contrast with the first, more than twenty years ago. Vir Singh was then over sixty and a legendary figure. He had become one in his twenties with the publication of his first novel, *Sundari.* It is hard to believe that a man like him should have become the subject of such fierce controversy amongst a people who admired his writing, were grateful to him for what he was doing, and above all, who never joined a faction against another or said one word of disparagement about anyone. The main criticism was against his allowing people to worship him—which indeed thousands did—and his being surrounded by a circle which consisted largely of the wealthier sections of Sikh society. Young people were highly critical of him on these scores; I counted myself amongst them and not only refused to touch his feet but made fun of people who made obeisance before him. Yet I lived to make my obeisance, touch his feet and give him the respect I would give no other living man.

A man of Vir Singh's poetic genius and religious bent of mind would get little chance to escape the attentions of people in quest of spiritual values. From the age of twenty-six he became the central figure in Sikh affairs—and in a subtle way was far more powerful than the politicians and ministers who hit the headlines of newspapers every other day. This for two reasons. He was the man who brought about a renaissance of the Punjabi language after a virtual lapse of more than two centuries. Vir Singh also gave a fillip to the Sikh religion. Through his weekly journal, *Khalsa Samachar*, his books, *Guru Nanak Chamatkar*, *Kalgidhar Chamatkar* and many tracts which were given away in the millions he told the story of the Sikh Gurus, their teachings and their achievements. His novels *Sundari*, *Bijai Singh* and *Satwant Kaur*, which make dull and didactic reading today, sold in the thousands because they gave the Sikhs of fifty years ago exactly what they wanted: an assurance of the excellence of their faith, a pride in the valour of their forefathers and a confidence in the traditions of orthodoxy handed down by the Gurus. Although Vir Singh was not the founder of the Singh Sabha movement which espoused these causes, he was more responsible for its achievements than all the other members put together.

LEARNING AND HUMILITY

Vir Singh's reaction to the adoration that came his way was that of a modest man with a deep-seated sense of humility. He was the one man who answered the Gita's definition of vidya vinaya sampanne—great humility which comes of great learning. As people clamoured to see him and hear him speak, he became less and less visible. He never appeared at public functions, he never made a speech, he never allowed anyone to photograph him. Not one of his many books carried his name on its jacket and he had written more than any Indian dead or alive: his complete works would be bulkier than the entire set of the *Encyclopaedia Britannica*. They represent over sixty years of uninterrupted writing of six to eight hours a day.

The sense of humility never left him and appears like a refrain in many of his verses. The achievement is never that of the human being but that of the Maker who in his compassion chose him to be his instrument of expression. Sometimes this sense becomes that of being used—or in the effeminate masochistic extreme of being misused—for a divine purpose:

Thou didst pluck and tear me from the branch
Held me, breathed the fragrance
And cast me away
Thus discarded
Trodden underfoot and mingled with the dust
All I remember—and with gratitude—
Is the memory of the touch.

The first time I saw him at a public meeting was at a kavi sammelan in Sargodha where he sat obscurely mixed up with the people. A young boy had recited a stirring ballad which had moved Vir Singh and he had asked to meet him. The news went around the 20,000-member audience that Vir Singh was amongst them; they clamoured for his darshan because all had read or heard of him, very few had seen him. He was almost dragged to the microphone on the platform. Roars of 'Sat Sri Akal' lasting a good fifteen minutes greeted him. All he could do was to fold his hands and mumble: 'Wahe Guruji Ka Khalsa, Wahe Guruji Ki Fateh.' Whichever way he turned thousands of heads bowed to touch the ground like a field of corn bending to the breeze. No Sikh since the Sikh Gurus could have known worship the way it was offered to Vir Singh; no one deserved it more.

NO CONVENTIONAL SAINT

Vir Singh did not look, live or behave like a conventional saint. He was not lean or ascetic in appearance; he was of medium height, of stocky build and with a long flowing beard. He dressed well and lived like an upper-class bourgeois person in a large house with a larger garden. He was married with two daughters. He kept an excellent table. He was a strict vegetarian and a great stickler for cleanliness. All fruits and vegetables were regularly washed in potassium permanganate before they were cooked or consumed in his house. He had a great love for his garden and grew exotic strains of citrus—grapefruit and Malta oranges. His favourite flower was the narcissus, which blossomed in profusion in beds about his windows.

He was not indifferent to money; his poems fetched larger royalties than those of any other poet. Both he and his scholarly brother had a dominant voice in the affairs of a bank.

Vir Singh was hardly known outside the Sikh community ten years ago. It was only after the conferment of doctorates from universities, nomination to the Punjab Council, the Sahitya Akademi Award for 'Mere Sayan Jeo' and the Padma Bhushan that other people got to hear of him. That was not surprising, for although he was not narrow-minded in his outlook and had close associations with innumerable Hindus and a lifelong friendship with a Muslim doctor, Sikhs and the Sikh religion were his only preoccupation.

FAITH IN SIKHISM

The dominant impression that Vir Singh left on his visitors was one of gentleness. He spoke softly and what he said had the soothing quality of a salve. Here, again, was the mysterious something which he attributed to the Guru in his writing and possessed in good measure himself:

> As a cloud ambling along
> For a moment tarries
> To cast a cool shadow on the parched earth
> And send a welcome shower.

Vir Singh has gone but in his case it certainly is the casting off of worn-out clothes and donning new ones. Even while he lived, people knew him only through his writings which will live forever. Wherever the Punjabi language is spoken, there Vir Singh's name will be spoken too. And whenever the Sikhs begin to doubt their faith, there will be Vir Singh's spirit to inspire them and beckon them back to the fold.

(Undated)

NEED TO RE-EDIT HINDU SCRIPTURES

If we continue to regard our ancient religious texts as the words of God and treat them with superstitious awe rather than as words of wisdom applicable to a particular period in history, we have little chance of equating them with reason and the needs of modern society. Arun Shourie, executive editor of the *Indian Express,* examines the Upanishads, the Gita and the Brahma Sutras along with commentaries on them and concludes that the only one who had the courage to sift the grain from the chaff was Mahatma Gandhi.

It takes courage even in secular India to impugn the sanctity of the sacred texts. Although most scholars of religion would agree in private that there is a lot of claptrap in all the sacred books, and that if they were to be re-edited it would enhance their spiritual appeal, few have shown the temerity to say so in public.

This is understandable because for centuries purveyors of religion have dinned it into our ears that these texts are the words of God, transmitted to humanity through the prophets. And woe betide anyone who tampered with a single word. Consequently, instead of being read as books of wisdom or as codes of practical ethics, they have been treated with superstitious awe and their words endowed with superhuman potency.

The best that reformers could do was to interpret them in different ways, often bending the original text beyond recognition. As far as Hinduism is concerned, sanctity has been accorded to the Vedas, the Upanishads, the Bhagavad Gita and the Brahma Sutras. They have always been regarded by orthodox Hindus as the words of God. Having declared them divinely immutable, the best the commentators—from Shankara, Ramanuja down to Swami Dayananda, Tilak, Ramakrishna, Sri Aurobindo and Ramana Maharshi—could do was to either ignore the contradictions or get around them by tortuous explanations.

As I have said at the outset, the one man who had both the honesty and the courage to separate the grains of truth from the chaff of meaningless verbosity was Mahatma Gandhi. All this has been very painstakingly brought out by Arun Shourie in his treatise, *Hinduism: Essence and Consequence*. The thesis he propounds is at once scholarly, novel, daring and exhilarating. Shourie has rendered significant service to Gandhi, Hinduism and India.

Shourie starts with the principal Upanishads and examines what they have had to say on the three topics that concern all religions, namely man's relations with his Maker, man's relations with his fellow men, and man's relations with himself, i.e. his 'inner self' or his conscience. The texts laid much greater emphasis on defining God (Brahman) and his identity with man's inner self (Atman) than on his rights and duties vis-a-vis other men. And, for some obscure reason, stilling the mind by emptying it of all other thoughts except the one in which the self-that-is-God became the be-all and the end-all of a Hindu's religious exercise. 'Even as foam is produced in a vessel containing liquid by churning, so also it is only from churning the mind that various doubts arise,' says the Trisikhi Brahmana Upanishad. The overall test is 'to bring this fickle monkey of a mind, this wayward damsel, this street dog under control'. The Upanishads present 'a veritable cafeteria' of means to achieve this end. From overcoming desires by stilling the sense organs ('temptations', says the Maitrayaniya Upanishad, 'are mere harlots entering the mind') we descend to magical mantras (above all the Gayatri), repetition of Om, wearing rudraksha malas, ablutions with cow's urine, and bathing (preferably dying) on the banks of the Ganga to attain moksha.

COMFORTING KARMA

Once a person is enjoined to concentrate all his mental facilities on himself, it is only natural that other men receive little consideration; they are just so much flesh, bone, bile, phlegm and excreta. The world is maya, an illusion. So is suffering. The best you can do about it is to ignore it or to explain it away as karma. The ultimate goal of man's earthly endeavour should be to break out of the cycle of birth-death-rebirth and merge back into Brahma: in this endeavour, maintain the texts, gyan (knowledge) yields better dividends than karma (action or good works). Sankara applauds the complete withdrawal from worldly strife (sanyas) even before completing the earlier stages of life as a student and as a householder.

Shourie maintains that 'the principal concern of the authors of the Upanishads, Brahma Sutras and the Gita was to dilute people's obsession with rituals, sacrifices etc.' He goes on to say that the 'tit for tat attitude by which the people expected rewards for the rituals and sacrifices was not just bad for the people, it was a severe embarrassment for the priests too. They had to continuously answer for the promised rewards that hadn't turned up.' But the doctrine of nishkama karma (work without concern for reward) came in very handy. Shourie reproduces the kind of dialogue that could have taken place:

'Panditji,' I say, 'when I asked you over to help perform that elaborate sacrifice, you said, quoting the Vedas, that I would get such and thus in return. I haven't received anything like that, you know.'

'But you mean, my son, that you launched upon the sacrifice, hankering after its rewards? That's precisely the reason why the fruit is delayed. Does the Gita not tell us, my son, that we should perform all works without any desire for the fruit?'

'Of course, Panditji. But I did not hanker after the rewards in that sense.'

'Well, if you did not, my son, then there is no problem. You have done the good deed. The deed itself is your reward. And I can assure you, you *will* reap the reward. Does Krishna himself in the second discourse itself not say, "There is no loss of effort here?" If not now, then later, my son. If not in this life, then in the next, my son. But remember the cardinal rule: do as the Shastras say, never hanker after the results.'

Shourie contends that the teachings of the Upanishads are not an adequate foundation for ethics because not only can transgressions be overcome in various easy ways, there is also the assurance that one does not incur sin as long as the deed is done with detachment. So the responsibility shifts from the doer to the Absolute.

The Brahma Sutras, discussed under the caption 'Verbal Vomit', are concerned more with absurdities than with profundities—the sort of footling disputation that Lenin decried about the Devil being green or yellow.

So we come to the Gita, the most sacred of the sacred Hindu texts. The commentaries on it are as diverse as the people who read it: Sankara, Tilak, Gandhi and even Godse. 'The Gita', says Shourie, 'is like the Upanishads, a loosely structured work. A topic is taken up and left, another intervenes only to be overshadowed by the next.' This gave ample scope for placing whatever interpretation suited the temperament of the times. Sankara and Ramakrishna read the message of renunciation—tyag—as its central theme. For Tilak, the Gita propounds nothing but undiluted karma yoga—'nothing happens till something is done.' Gandhi refused to believe that Krishna was actually exhorting Arjuna to wage war against his kinsmen and considered Kurukshetra a purely symbolic battlefield between good and evil. He extracted ahimsa as its real message. Godse must have thought that as long as he was doing what he did in the spirit of nishkama karma he was absolved of all guilt. 'Detachment, then, exempts one and absolute detachment exempts absolutely,' remarks Shourie.

MONOPOLIZING GURUS

Shourie points out that the Westernized elite tend to dismiss Gandhi as a faddist and as a traditionalist without realizing that 'like a true revolutionary who looked into the people's psyche', he beat the orthodox Hindus and Jains at their most vulnerable points. Although he had no pretensions to scholarship, what he had read 'convinced him that the texts, though useful, could never be elevated to being [the] final arbiter'. He rejected both the literal interpretations and the authority of the gurus who often claimed monopoly over sacred knowledge. He used to say that the texts suffered from a process of 'double distillation' because they came to us through a human prophet 'and then passed through a second distillation by commentators'. He stated, 'Categorically, I would reject all scriptural authority if it is in conflict with sober reason or the dictates of the heart. Authority sustains and ennobles the weak when it is the handiwork of reason, but it degrades them when it supplants reason sanctified by the still, small voice within... blind worship of authority is a sign of weakness of mind...' Shourie goes on to contrast the attributes of Sankara and Gandhi. Where Sankara is preoccupied with the scriptures, Gandhi is preoccupied with life and 'the actual struggles that the masses must wage. Here is the difference between scholastic disputation and life, between exegetical polemics and real struggles.'

THE GITA, THE WORK OF A POET, NOT OF GOD

Gandhi regarded the Gita as the work of a poet, not of God and maintained that its meaning changed with the times. Thus, he concludes that sacrifice could not mean killing of animals nor sanyas mean giving up actions. He went even further than that by exhorting the spinning of the charkha as a 'means of universal service in this age'. Gandhi rejected whatever did not suit him. Of soma juice, mentioned in the sacred texts, he disclaims all knowledge. He was categorical in his denunciation of caste, as sanctified by the Gita and the Manu Shastra. He said 'Brahmanism is the culmination of other varnas just as the head is the culmination of the body. It means capacity for superior service, not superior status. The moment superior status is arrogated, it becomes worthy of being trampled underfoot.'

Shourie rightly concludes: 'Here at last is a man who has the calm self-assurance to claim as much authority as the texts, the gurus and the saints on the basis of one single thing—his own practice... Gandhi has been the greatest emancipator in our history thus far and the most original social thinker that we have had since the Buddha... his practice, for instance, contrasted so very sharply from the practice of the Ramana Maharshis and the Ramakrishnas. They are preoccupied with realizing their "self" and this quest leads them to an inner-directed introspective endeavour. Gandhi too talks of realizing his "self". But in his lexicon the word and its import have been transformed by subtle changes. He convinces himself that he can realize this self only when other selves are liberated from their suffering. For him, therefore, the means to self-realization is no longer an obsessively inward-directed effort; rather the means is service to one's fellow man.'

(1979)

CONTROLLING THE URGE TO BACKCHAT

For many years when I was young and believed in resolutions to improve myself, my New Year's resolve used to be to not run people down behind their backs. I was in the habit of doing so and hated myself afterwards. Whatever I said somehow got known to the person I had maligned. When confronted by him or her, I had to deny what I had said and had reason to feel low in my self-estimation. I was able to check myself from talking about others behind their backs for a few days. I resumed the bad habit but somehow it got less and less on its own. I came to realize the truth of Guru Nanak's admonition:

> Nanak, phika boleeai
> Tan man phikka hoi
>
> (Nanak, if you speak ill of people
> Your body and mind will fall sick.)

The Guru's words can also be interpreted to apply to saying nasty things to people to their faces. Many people make it a point to say hurtful things to others and justify themselves by saying that they are merely speaking their minds. When in return they get more than they give, a slanging match results in which both participants get hurt while others enjoy the spectacle.

Another of my annual resolutions was that no matter how grave the provocation I would not lose my temper. My father had a short temper; his father was even more ill-tempered. My father never used bad language but being overworked, he was impatient and inclined to snap at everyone. We were terrified of him and kept out of his way as much as we could. In later years of his life, he mellowed a great deal and I looked forward to joining him in the evenings for a sundowner. However, I could never get over my allergy towards people with short tempers. Incidents of people snubbing me still rankle in my mind. I have no forgiveness for them. I write off people who lose their temper with me forever and no amount of their trying to make amends makes any difference in my attitude towards them.

According to our ancient scriptures, Hindu and Sikh, krodh (anger) is as serious a shortcoming as kama (lust), lobh (greed), moh (attachment) and ahankar (arrogance). They exhort us to overcome them in order to achieve moksha (salvation). They do not tell us how we go about getting the better of them. As far as anger is concerned, people have their own formulae: 'When roused to anger, count ten before answering' or 'Swallow the insult and keep your mouth shut'. There is no doubt that a person who loses his cool loses the argument. Another school of thought is that it is better to let off steam and get over with it because if you contain your anger, your blood pressure will rise and you may get peptic ulcers.

I have evolved my own formula to get anger out of my system. I say nothing to the person who has insulted or snubbed me but when I narrate the incident to my friends later, I let loose a torrent of the choicest abuse in Punjabi and Hindustani—I have a large repertoire of filthy words in four languages—and purge myself of anger. I even feel exhilarated at having scored over my traducer by saying nothing to him or her and cleansing my system by letting out the accumulated venom in front of third parties who thoroughly enjoy my outburst.

(2001)

SANGAM OF RELIGIONS

When I was a child of about four living in a tiny village with my grandmother, she taught me my first prayer. I was scared of the dark and prone to having nightmares. She told me that whenever I was frightened, I should recite the following lines by Guru Arjan:

> Taatee vau na laagaee, Peer-Brahma sarnaee
> Chowgird hamaarey Ram-kar, dukh lagey na bhaee
>
> (No ill-winds touch you, the great Lord your protector be around you
> Lord Rama has drawn a protective line, Brother, no harm will come to thee.)

Being young, innocent and having infinite trust in my granny's assurances, these lines worked like magic. Later, I discovered that most Sikh children were taught the same lines even before they learnt other prayers. The hymn had four more lines:

> Satgur poora bhetiya, jis banat banaaee
> Ram naam aukhad deeya, eka liv laayee
> Raakh liye tin raakhan har, sabh biaadh mitaayee
> Kaho Nanak kirpa bhaee, Prabhu bhaye sahaaee
>
> (The true guru was revealed in his fullness, the one who did all create,
> He gave the name of Rama as medicine, in him alone I repose my faith.
> He saved all who deserve to be saved, he removes all worries of the mind.
> Sayeth Nanak, God became my helper, he was kind.)

Mark the Hindu terminology in this short prayer: Peer, Brahma, Ram-kaar, Ram-naam, and Prabhu. As a matter of fact, a painstaking scholar counted the number of times the name of God appears in the Adi Granth. The total comes to around 16,000. Of these, over 14,000 are of Hindu origin: Hari, Ram, Govind, Narayan, Krishna, Murari, Madhav, Vithal etc. There is also a sizeable number of Islamic names for God: Allah, Rehman, Rahim, Kareem, etc. The purely Sikh coinage 'Wahe Guru' appears only sixteen times.

The point I am trying to make is all religions take a lot from other religions with which they come into contact: there is not a single religion in the world which has not borrowed some concept or the other from another–some of its vocabulary and even its ritual. In the Judaic family of religions—Judaism, Christianity and Islam—there is plenty of evidence of wholesale borrowing. A good example is Islam. Its monotheism exists in Judaism and Christianity. Its five daily prayers have roughly the same names as those of Jews; its greeting salaam alaikum is a variation of the Jewish shalom aleichem; turning to Mecca for namaaz is based on the practice of Jews turning to Jerusalem for saying their prayers; their food inhibitions which consider pork unclean is similar to that of the Jews, halal is the same as Jewish kosher, the custom of circumcising male children, sunnat, is also Jewish.

The intermingling of faiths is much more in evidence in the Hindu family of religions: Hinduism, Jainism, Buddhism, and Sikhism. All share belief in karma, the cycle of birth-death-rebirth, meditation etc. Needless to say, they also share much of their religious terminology. Since Sikhism was the last of these major religions and the only one to come into contact with Islam, it is the only one which took a lot of the terminology of Islam from Sufi saints.

When the thekedars (contractors or purveyors) of religion claim that their faith owes nothing to the others and is, therefore, purest of the pure, it makes me laugh at their ignorance.

(2001)

LAND-GRABBING IN THE NAME OF GOD

Israel Zangwill wrote an amusing story set in rural Poland about a very poor young Jewish couple who lived outside a village and eked out a miserable living, selling firewood to the villagers. Near Christmas time the demand for firewood increased, so the couple was able to earn a little more than usual. While the Christian village was preparing to celebrate with lavish eating and drinking, the young Jewish couple decided to celebrate in their own way. On Christmas Eve, the young wife went out in the snow to get some more firewood for their hearth. She came to a pond which was frozen hard. She had not bathed for several days. Knowing what her husband had in mind, she took off her clothes, smashed the ice and jumped into the pool. She heard men's voices at a distance coming towards the pool. They were two farmers out shooting birds to add to their Christmas fare. The girl jumped out of the pool, gathered her clothes and ran naked to her hut. The farmers saw the figure of a naked woman running across the snow and vanish in the mist. Who could it be on Christmas Eve except the Virgin Mary? The story spread in the village. A widow whose son had been stricken with paralysis took him to the pool and dumped him in the icy water. The shock cured the child of his ailment. A bishop came to investigate and proclaimed the water of the pond to be holy. It became a place of pilgrimage and miracle cures. Soon a cathedral was built near it. The Jewish couple went into business selling water from the pond in small bottles. They made a lot of money and became rich.

Zangwill's story is being reproduced all over our country with unscrupulous people grabbing public land in the name of their deities. I have witnessed a few instances in Kasauli and Delhi. The highest point in Kasauli was for some reason given the name Monkey Point. As a boy I often climbed to the top. There was nothing there except a pile of stones. You got a spectacular view of the plains with the Sutlej River flowing through them. Then the Indian Air Force moved in. It built a lot of very ugly flats at the base of Monkey Point on what had once been Kasauli's favourite picnic spot. On the peak was installed a slab of stone smeared with bright red paint. Monkey Point became Hanuman Point. A story was circulated that Hanuman, after finding the sanjeevani booti, had put his foot down on this spot. So a temple came up. Now it has a full-time priest. People come from distant towns and make offerings of money, fruit and flowers. A few months ago, it received an important visitor, a minister more stupid than the usual run of ministers, who declared that a spot hallowed by the touch of the foot of Bajrang Bali should not be known as Monkey Point but Maan Kee Point. A Hindu bania of Kasauli has done better. There are a few Muslim graves in the town, one very close to the main bazaar. There are no permanent Muslim residents but some superstitious Hindu women were in the habit of making mannat at the graves. So he had the one near the bazaar given a coat of fresh green paint and spread the canard that it belonged to a pir sahib who granted the wishes of devotees. Now there is a stream of pilgrims making offerings at the tomb. The bania is doing good business. There are two other tombs which are due to be renovated with fresh paint and oil lamps. Like shopkeepers who have a chain of shops, our local bania owns a chain of Muslim tombs. Good income, no income tax.

In the last few years I have seen a proliferation of Hindu places of worship in the oddest of locations. One is along the wall of what was once Mr Jinnah's residence. It is on a side lane and all there was worth noticing was a huge peepul tree. Then the bole got a dab of saffron paint followed by a slab of stone with the statue of a deity. Now it is a wayside shrine. The whole area between the office of the BJP and the road has recently been taken over by some pandits to convert into a temple. Likewise, there are dozens of shrines along roads, on road-dividers, and just about every place not already occupied. People are too scared to demolish structures which have been sanctified by worshippers. The police is equally scared to take action lest it arouses communal frenzy. So the loot of public land in the name of God goes on unabated.

It needs men of determination to put an end to this menace. Some years ago a party of Nihang Sikhs sat down in the middle of a fairway of the Delhi Golf Club. They said one of them had dreamt that Guru Gobind Singh had desired that he build a gurdwara on the spot. They refused to listen to reason; the police refused to help the club out of its predicament. In sheer desperation, late one night when the Nihangs were deep in bhang-induced sleep, club employees led by a few intrepid members swooped down on them, picked up all their utensils, bedding etc., and threw the lot out on the road and shut the club gates. No more was heard of the Nihangs.

(2002)

THE AGNOSTIC

'God is a gas balloon. Or that red rubber ball you kick around in your garden!' exclaimed the Agnostic. Then 'God' descended on the Agnostic. Or was it a mere coincidence?

The argument went on the lines it had gone many times before.

'So you don't believe in God! Is it only for the sake of an argument or do you really and truly do not?' asked the host. 'So help you God!'

'No, I really and truly do not believe in God. So help me Satan!' answered the visitor.

'Then where does all this come from?' demanded the host, warming up and waving his arms around. 'These trees, these human beings, these animals, this world and everything that's in it?' Being a politician, he was given to rhetoric. His family always voted for him.

'I don't know,' replied the visitor. And before they could checkmate him with a 'There!' he continued, 'Nor do you. Nor did any of your prophets and messiahs and avatars. Nor does anyone else. All your religions are a mumbo jumbo of children's fairy—'

'I know where everything comes from,' interrupted the ten-year-old son of the host who never let an argument go without voicing his opinion. 'Everything comes from God. So there!' He snapped his thumb and finger in the visitor's face. 'It's God, God, God. And if you believe in Satan, you have to believe in God.'

'Who said I believe in Satan! He is as much a creature of sick minds as God.' To make it simpler for the young lad, he added: 'Your God is a gas balloon—or like that red rubber ball you boys kick around in your garden.'

The family were aghast. 'Oh please! For God's sake, don't destroy my children's faith with this kind of blasphemy!' pleaded the hostess. 'I pay a Maulvi Sahib to come and teach them to read the Quran and say their prayers. And you ruin it all.'

She turned to her children: 'Don't you believe a word he says. Now go and do your homework. Off with you!'

The children were reluctant to go; a quarrel between elders was too good to be missed. But a bit of bribery and lots of cajoling made them get up and drag their feet to their room. The youngest one left with a parting exclamation and a laugh: 'God is a red rubber ball.'

'Look what you have done!' despaired the hostess. 'They will say this kind of thing in their school—a Catholic institution—and be thrown out. They will not fast during Ramzan and stop saying their prayers. They will not have any faith left—not even as a prop or a crutch to fall back on. Do you want them to become dropouts and misfits?'

The visitor continued needling her. 'In that case you should not expose your children to people like me. Don't invite me to your home; just have your Maulvi Sahibs and Catholic fathers and superstitious God-fearing uncles, aunts and cousins stuff their brains with all the poppycock of Allah-in-Heaven-Adam-Eve-Day-of-Judgement-Reincarnation-Nirvana. Don't let them think, okay?'

'Achha! Achha! No need to get so worked up,' said the host to restore peace. 'Let's go for a walk. That'll help you both to cool down.'

They strolled in the garden. The visitor tried to make up to his hostess. 'The argument always goes the same way. I suppose it always has. To wit:

Myself when young did eagerly frequent
Doctor and Saint, and heard great argument
About it and about: but ever more
Came out by the same door as in I went.

'Maybe!' she responded graciously. 'But I still stick to my point: I cannot dream that this watch exists but has no watchmaker.'

'Whoever said that?'

'Voltaire. But the analogy does not apply. We know the world exists, unless it is one grand delusion—maya—as some Hindus and Sikhs believe, but we do not know anything about the World Maker. Even assuming there is a Creator, there is no reason to worship him. There is more evil in the world than good. It is best to observe silence. This is the door to which no one has found the key, the veil beyond which no one can see. It's more honest to say "I do not know" than posit theories which go contrary to reason. I neither know that there is a God, nor know that there is no God. That's why I call myself an agnostic.'

'Sure, sure!' said the host condescendingly. 'You are welcome to your lack of belief. But leave alone those who would rather believe till it is positively proved that their beliefs have been wrong. Live and let live. And now let's talk of something else.'

But the visitor persisted: 'What I cannot stand is religiosity, the asinine worship of miracle men who are no better than common jugglers churning up age-old and unproven theories of God, Soul, Love and what-have-you! And the millions of asses who get taken in by them!'

'It's God we are discussing, not miracle men,' intervened the hostess. 'What amazes me,' she added, 'is that a man who disdains all belief in the supernatural should be so obsessed with the subject of God as you are. You provoke it as a man with a sore tooth provokes pain by feeling the tooth with his tongue. Perhaps in your strong protestations is an element of faith which you refuse to admit—like a man shouting in the dark to give himself courage.'

'That's true,' agreed the host. 'Reminds me of those lines from Francis Thompson:

I fled Him, down the nights and down the days;
I fled Him, down the arches of the years;
I fled Him, down the labyrinthine ways
Of my own mind; and in the midst of tears
I hid from Him, and under running laughter...

But with unhurrying chase,
And unperturbed pace.
Deliberate speed, majestic instancy,
They beat—and a Voice beat
More instant than the Feet—
All things betray thee, who betrayest Me.

He will catch up with you one day even if you denigrate him as the red rubber ball.'

It was time for dinner. They returned to the house. The hostess clapped her hands and called out: 'To the table, children!'

As soon as everyone was seated and the hostess began to heap food on her children's plates, the little fellow began to giggle: 'God is a red rubber ball!'

'Let's make plans for tomorrow.' The hostess tried to change the subject.

'Gas balloon—no my red rubber ball...'chuckled the little brat.

'Stop that now!' admonished the hostess. 'Not another word or I'll really blow up.'

God was not mentioned at the table that night. But the next morning at breakfast the youngsters were eager to get their parents and the visitor to restart the argument. The little one picked up the red rubber ball and put it in the visitor's lap with a meaningful remark: 'You take this.' His mother glowered at him. 'Remember, any more of that and I will call off the picnic.'

◆

It was a Sunday morning. Late monsoon time. Clouds rolling overhead cast deep shadows on the earth. Showers came down as suddenly as they went to let the sun stream through and span the sky with rainbows. 'Lovely day for a picnic in the park,' said the hostess.

They drove to the park. The children took the red rubber ball with them. They began to toss it at each other, then into the trees and waited to catch it as it bounced off the branches. The host and hostess showed the visitor the newly laid-out rose garden.

They came to a massive peepul tree. The oldest boy tossed the ball high into the air to let it drop on the tree. It soared up and came downwards, bouncing from one branch to another. The boys waited for it with hands outstretched. The ball bounced upwards off the lowest branch, came down and was embedded in a Y-shaped cleft. 'Oh, oh, oh,' groaned the lads, 'the ball is stuck in the tree.'

They spent the next half hour hurling stones and sticks to dislodge the ball. Their father's patience came to an end. 'We can't spend the rest of the morning trying to get the ruddy ball down! Let's go and have something to drink.'

The boys abandoned their attempts. But their spirits were dampened. They went to the aerated water stall and sipped their drinks without enjoying them. 'Arrey baba!' protested their mother. 'It's only a rubber ball! You don't have to look as if the world has come to an end! I'll buy you another one.'

It did not change the boys' mood. Neither did the plates of potato chips, tomato ketchup and the ice creams. After an hour, the party wended its way back through the park towards the car.

They came under the peepul tree. The red ball was still firmly embedded in the cleft of the branches. They all looked up: 'It's still there.' This time no one made any attempt to dislodge it.

The visitor friend tried to cheer them up. He proclaimed very loudly: 'All right. If that red rubber ball drops into my hands now, I'll believe there is a God.'

A gentle gust of breeze swayed the branches and the red rubber ball fell neatly into the visitor's hands.

They stood in silence, gaping at each other.

'That will teach you a lesson!' hissed the hostess.

'Damn!' swore the Agnostic.

(1972)

GURU GOLWALKAR

There are some people against whom you build up malice without knowing them. Guru Golwalkar had long been at the top of my hate list because I could not forget the RSS's role in communal riots, the assassination of the Mahatma, the talk of changing India from a secular to a Hindu state! However, as a journalist, I could not resist the chance of meeting him.

I expected to run into a cordon of uniformed swayamsevaks. There are none, not even plainclothes CID to take down the number of my car. It is a middle-class apartment with an appearance of puja going on inside—rows of sandals outside, fragrance of agarbatti, bustle of women behind the scenes, the tinkle of utensils and crockery. In a small room sit a dozen men in spotless white kurtas and dhotis—all looking newly washed as only Maharashtrian Brahmins manage to do. And Guru Golwalkar–a frail man in his mid-sixties, black hair curling to his shoulders, a moustache covering his mouth, a wispy grey beard dangling down his chin. An unerasable smile and dark eyes twinkling through his bifocals. He looks like an Indian Ho Chi Minh. For a man who had only recently undergone surgery for breast cancer he looks remarkably fit and cheerful.

Being a guru, I feel he may expect a chela-like obeisance. He does not give me a chance. As I bend to touch his feet he grasps my hand in his bony fingers and pulls me down on the seat beside him. 'I am very glad to meet you,' he says. 'I have been wanting to do so for some time.' His Hindi is very shuddh.

'Me too,' I reply clumsily. 'Ever since I read your *Bunch of Letters.*'

'*Bunch of Thoughts*,' he corrects me. He does not want to know my views on it. He takes one of my hands in his and pats it. 'So?' he looks enquiringly at me.

'I don't know where to begin. I am told you shun publicity and your organization is secret.'

'It is true we do not seek publicity but there is nothing secret about us. Ask me anything you want to.'

'I read about your movement in Jack Curran's *The RSS and Hindu Militarism*. He says...'

'It is a biased account,' interrupts Guruji. 'Unfair, inaccurate—he misquoted me and many others. There is no militarism in our movement. We value discipline—which is a different matter.' I tell him that I had read an article describing Curran as the head of CIA operations in Europe and Africa. 'I would never have suspected it,' I say very naively, 'I have known him for twenty years.'

Guruji beams a smile at me. 'This doesn't surprise me at all,' he says. I do not know whether the remark is a comment on Curran being CIA or my naiveté.

'There is one thing which bothers me about the RSS. If you permit me, I will put it as bluntly as I can.'

'Go ahead!'

'It is your attitude towards the minorities, particularly the Christians and the Muslims.'

'We have nothing against the Christians except their methods of gaining converts. When they give medicines to the sick or bread to the hungry, they should not exploit the situation by propagating their religion to those people. I am glad there is a move to make the Indian churches autonomous and independent of Rome.'

'What about the Muslims?'

'What about them?'

I have no doubt in my mind that the dual loyalties that many Muslims have towards both India and Pakistan is due to historical factors for which Hindus are as much to blame as they. It also stems from a feeling of insecurity that they have been made to suffer since Partition. In any case, one cannot hold the entire community responsible for the wrongs of a few.

'Guruji, there are six crore Indian Muslims here with us.' I get eloquent. 'We cannot eliminate them, we cannot drive them out, we cannot convert them. This is their home. We must reassure them—make them feel wanted. Let us win them over with love. This should be an article of—'

'I would reverse the order,' he interrupts. 'As a matter of fact

I would say the only right policy towards Muslims is to win their loyalty by love.'

I am startled. Is he playing with words? Or does he really mean what he says? He qualifies his statement: 'A delegation of the Jamaat-i-Islami came to see me. I told them that Muslims must forget that they ruled India. They should not look upon foreign Muslim countries as their homeland. They must join the mainstream of Indianism.'

'How?'

'We should explain things to them. Sometimes one feels angry with Muslims for what they do, but then Hindu blood never harbours ill will for very long. Time is a great healer. I am an optimist and feel that Hinduism and Islam will learn to live with each other.'

Tea is served. Guruji's glass mug provides a diversion. I ask him why he doesn't drink the beverage out of porcelain like the rest of us. He smiles. 'I have always taken it in this mug, I take it with me wherever I go.' His closest companion, Dr Thatte, who has dedicated his life to the RSS, explains: 'Porcelain wears off and exposes the clay beneath. Clay can harbour germs.'

I return to my theme.

'Why do you pin your faith on religion when most of the world is turning irreligious and agnostic?'

'Hinduism is on firm ground because it has no dogma. It has had agnostics before, it will survive the wave of irreligiousness better than any other religious system.'

'How can you say that? The evidence is the other way. The only religions which are standing firm and even increasing their hold on the people are based on dogma—Catholicism, and more than Catholicism, Islam.'

'It is a passing phase. Agnosticism will overtake them, it will not overtake Hinduism. Ours is not a religion in the dictionary sense of the word; it is dharma, a way of life. Hinduism will take agnosticism in its stride.'

I have taken more than half an hour of Guruji's time. He shows no sign of impatience. When I ask for leave, he again grasps my hands to prevent me from touching his feet.

Was I impressed? I admit I was. He did not try to persuade me to his point of view. He made me feel that he was open to persuasion. I accepted his invitation to visit him in Nagpur and see things for myself. Maybe I can bring him around to making Hindu-Muslim unity the main aim of his RSS. Or am I being a simple-minded Sardarji?

(1972)

BHAGWAN SHRI NEELKANTHA TATHAJI

The resemblance to Satya Sai Baba is striking: the same beehive mop of fuzzy hair on the head, the same bright eyes that hold you, the same gentle smile, the same saffron robes that drape him from the shoulders to the feet. He performs similar kinds of miracles—waves his hands in the air and produces vibhuti—his followers say that he can heal the sick—one man claims that he was brought back to life after his heart had stopped beating. This man of miracles is thirty-seven-year-old Bhagwan Shri Neelkantha Tathaji, described by his followers as 'master, guide, guru and God-incarnate'.

I had been seeing advertisements in the papers announcing the arrival in our city of Bhagwan Shri Neelkantha Tathaji. People who desired darshan were invited to an apartment in a very upper-class residential locality. I was taken there by a Parsi couple, both bhakts of Neelkantha Tathaji. The large hall was full of worshippers chanting hymns: all well-dressed and upper-middle class. On a dais was an empty chair draped in silks. Beside it was another one with a large coloured portrait of the Baba, a garland around its frame and a dozen joss sticks sending up spirals of incense.

The Baba made his appearance. Everyone made obeisance, many people touched his feet. He took his seat on the dais and joined in the hymn-singing: Om Namah Shivaya, Om Namo Narayanaya. There were salutations to Lakshmi, Ganapati and to all the other gods of the pantheon—Sarva Dharmaya Namaskarah. He performed the aarti, waving a salver of oil lamps. The tempo of singing and clapping of hands came to a climax and ended abruptly. Neelkantha Tathaji retired to his room.

Six of us were invited to a private audience in his bedroom. We sat on the floor at his feet. He spoke to us. His Hindi was not very good and he often turned to one of his disciples to get the Hindi equivalent of a Telugu word or phrase. He told us he was one of five brothers—the sons of a poor farmer. When it came to a division of property, all he got was a few bushels of jowar. He asked that his ailing father be given to him as part of his patrimony.

When did the 'spirit' descend on him? He did not know the precise moment but other people noticed some strange phenomenon about him. When he put his hand on the forehead of a man down with fever, the fever left him. When he touched the gangrenous leg of someone on his way to hospital to have it amputated, the gangrene disappeared. A disciple sitting behind me whispered: 'My heart had stopped beating, I was dead. The Baba gave me a second life. Can't you see he is divine? See the light around his head.' Did I see a halo round the Baba's head?

HIS TOUCH TRANSFORMS

He asked me to come near him. I edged forward. He rubbed his thumb on his palm and dropped a pinch of ash in my hand. He repeated the gesture—a brown berry rudraksha appeared in his hand. 'Wear it around your neck,' he advised me. He pinned a badge with his picture on my shirt, gave me one to fix on my ear and slipped a ring (with his picture) on my finger. My friends had brought a basketful of fruit for him. He proceeded to distribute it to everyone. 'But this is for you,' protested the lady. He replied: 'What I have touched becomes prasad.' And gave her an apple and a banana from her basket. He invited us to his ashram, Om Nagar, in the Kurnool district of Andhra Pradesh, for his daughter's wedding next December, blessed us and gave us leave.

Shri Neelkantha Tathaji is an unsophisticated, unpretentious man possessed of magnetic power to draw people towards him. He is a source of comfort to his followers, and those who believe in the supranormal may find in him another man of miracles.

(1972)

GURUDEV MUKTANANDA AT VAJRESHWARI

It is only fifty miles from Bombay, but a thousand miles away from its noisy crowds and stench. I surveyed the scene from a hilltop. Rectangles of brown fields with paddy stubble like an unshaven chin. A ring of hills with names that tinkle like temple bells: Mandagani towers up in the north, Mawlai from where the sun rises, Tungareshwar where it sets. And running through the broad valley, like a silver thread, the stream Tejasa. The teak has shed its broad leaves, the peepul wears its new pink foliage, silk-cotton buds are ready to explode, the flame of the forest is in full bloom. As lovely a place to recharge your physical batteries as you can see anywhere. My journey was however undertaken to see if there was a spark left in my spiritual battery. I had gone to see Baba Muktananda.

Many friends protest, 'We've had enough of bhagwans and swamis from your predecessor. If you are going religious in your dotage, you don't have to inflict it on your readers.' No, I am not going religious. But I cannot keep away from men who are. Their experiences are different from mine. They live in another world. I want to know about it. I am curious; curiosity is my profession.

In the last fortnight I have met Balyogeshwar. No, I did not ask him about his trouble with the Customs. I had an hour with Ma Yogashakti Saraswati. I have spent many evenings with the Krishna Consciousness people. But I had never been in an ashram. And Muktanandaji's hospice at Vajreshwari had been strongly recommended.

There are many kinds of ashrams. Gandhiji had his Tolstoy Farm and Sabarmati where his devotees lived in spartan simplicity raising their own food and spinning their own cloth. The emphasis was on work rather than on prayer. Jayaprakash Narayan has his—where it is all work and no prayer.

In Gurudev Muktanandaji's ashram, it is the other way round: more time is spent on prayer and meditation, less on work. It is a rich establishment. Lavish display of marble and silver, expensive carpets and furnishing, modern bungalow, kitchen garden, rose garden, orchards growing papaya, banana, chickoo and mango. And a black elephant, a very friendly tusker called Swami Vijayananda, who turns up his trunk at fodder but loves apples and imported chocolate.

Muktanandaji is unlike any other guru I have met. When he walked into his teak-panelled, air-conditioned reception room where I awaited him, it took me some time to realize I was in the presence of a man that hundreds of thousands worship as God-incarnate. Though his lungi and shirt were of sanyasi saffron, his woollen cap with a pom-pom on top and his dark glasses made him an incongruous figure. Though he sat on a sofa with brocade upholstery, he exuded an aura of humility and friendship I had not encountered before.

'I would like to ask you some questions,' I said.

'Certainly!' he replied. 'I'll answer them as best as I can. But why not look around the ashram first? Then come back and talk to me and anyone else you like.'

I was taken around the dormitories, the dining room and the library. All very neat and clean. I walked around the corridor-like meditation rooms and saw many men and women sitting straight-backed in padmasana pose, lost to the world.

Later in the afternoon, Muktanandaji came into the meditation room. He sent for his foreign disciples. Three Americans and a French girl joined us.

Muktanandaji is Mangalorean. He can speak Hindi and Marathi and not English.

'Why do people come to you?' I asked him in Hindi. He replied briefly: 'For different reasons. Some are unhappy, some disturbed, some curious.'

'What do they get from you?'

'They get peace of mind. Through meditation they learn how to know themselves and God who is in everyone.'

I don't give up. 'Is peace of mind the ultimate goal? It seems to me to be a selfish, self-centred ideal. A man should give more to others than to himself.'

'They do that too,' replied Muktanandaji. 'It's only after a person has found the divine in himself that he can become an integrated personality and be able to give the love that he has within him.'

His disciples take over. The Americans are Uma, Damyanti and Chandra—all with Hindu names. All young, attractive and voluble. 'We are not dropouts. We come from good families,' they say in turns but let slip information that they had been taking drugs or other palliatives against unhappiness.

'What now?' I ask them.

'I've never been happier. I am at peace with myself,' says one whose eyes sparkle with joy. I think her name is Damyanti.

'Peace never produced anything worthwhile; it is the restless agitation of the mind that has created the great works of art, music, science. These electric gadgets—fans, air conditioners, lights—all were invented by those who tortured their minds. The world is the richer for their sufferings.'

'We are so happy we could do without them.'

'That's no answer; what would the world be without scientific inventions, paintings, music?'

'We give the best of what we have. We can't all be Michelangelos and Beethovens.'

'But this meditation you set so much store by seems to me to be a kind of selfish indulgence and a waste of time. I'd rather read a good book. I'd rather sleep than keep awake with my eyes shut.'

There is laughter all round. Muktanandaji asks what has been said. Sri Yende, who is one of his close disciples, gives him a summary of the discussion. He nods his head approvingly and asks me to continue.

There is little doubt that this man has the capacity of putting everyone at ease; of making everyone feel he or she is someone very special. And he is utterly unpretentious. I have never felt closer to a holy man in so short a time. We continue our discussion till we reach an impasse over meditation versus work.

'Why don't you try it out?' says Uma, who edits their newsletter. 'It is hard to explain what it does—just as hard as it is to tell a person who has never eaten chocolate what chocolate tastes like.'

The seance is over. Professor Jain takes up the discussion. He cuts me down to size. 'Everyone does his work as best as he can. You edit the *Weekly*, Uma edits our newsletter. Both are equally important.' I acknowledge my error. He forgives me with a smile and continues. 'Shakespeare took many years to write his plays and poems; in seventeen days our Gurudev wrote *Chitshakti Vilas*. The play of consciousness. It is greater than anything Shakespeare ever wrote. It did not come out of any agitation of the mind but out of profound peace.'

The girls assure me that they are not escaping from their responsibilities. Although life in the ashram gives them peace and serenity, it is not easy. Getting up at 3.30 a.m. and the work, prayer and meditation is rigorous discipline.

'To what end?' I ask them in exasperation. 'I don't believe in God and I don't need him, so why should I go looking for him inside me?'

'You have more faith in you than you are willing to admit,' chorus the girls and repeat the challenge: 'Try it out and see for yourself. Come and stay in the ashram for a few days.'

'I'd find pretty girls like you very distracting.'

They laugh happily.

I take leave of Muktanandaji. I ask him to forgive me for the rude questions I have put to him and his devotees. He places his hand on my shoulder and smiles. 'They were not rude questions, they were honest. Come again.'

I will go again to Vajreshwari. Let others go there to recharge their spiritual batteries, I will go to see the flame of the forest in flower, breathe fresh mountain air and get reassurance from the Gurudev Muktanandaji that I am not as much of a rascal as I think I am.

(1973)

One morning my friend Virendra Luther of Polydor rang me up and in a very excited voice asked me, 'Do you remember my telling you about the Swamiji who has a copy of the Bhrigu Samhita? Well, he is with me and, believe it or not, he's found a page with your name on it. It's here right before my eyes.'

I recalled my earlier reaction to similar claims made on behalf of the Bhrigu Samhita. I had dismissed it with one word: 'Rubbish'. And when told of the number of cabinet ministers, chief ministers, chief justices, members of legislatures and other VIPs who regularly consulted it, I had said, 'I am neither surprised nor impressed. They are mentally sick morons.'

A few minutes later, Luther, looking as pleased as a cat that had swallowed a mouse, ushered in a very wizened and seemingly unperturbed Pandit Kundan Lal of Hoshiarpur. Panditji unpacked a bundle of parchments which was the Bhrigu Samhita: pages yellowed with age, perforated and written in faded black ink with a reed pen. He tucked his feet under him on the chair and found the page which applied to me. It read: 'On the so-and-so of so-and-so (dates of the Vikrami calendar) in a city beginning with the letter *B* beside the ocean at the hour of 11 a.m., a man named so-and-so will come to ask questions about himself.' Luther picked up the loose page and triumphantly held it for me to see. Yes, my name was there. I begged Panditji to translate what it said about me.

Apparently in my previous birth I had also been a non-believer in the occult and had suffered because of my lack of faith. Some of that unbelief had persisted into my present life and would continue to do so in the next. Beyond that he specified the exact time of my demise. Apparently I am to live up to 1999 and die a few months before the turn of the century.

Can those who believe in previous births explain how our numbers keep multiplying? Where were these additional people before their present births? I wish these samhitas would be subjected to scientific tests which determine the age of the paper and ink used. I also suggest that those who make their living by it be kept under scrutiny over a period to find out how and when people's names are inserted in their books of the future.

Was I impressed? Again, a one word comment: fiddlesticks.

The second encounter was with a young Swamiji. 'I don't know about other things,' said a friend who knew him. 'He had adverse reports in *Blitz* and some leftist papers. But he has powers of siddhi. You write three questions, without looking at the paper he will tell you what they are. He can cure diseases.' Apparently one of the owners of Bennett Coleman & Co., who had been afflicted with diabetes for many years, was miraculously rid of the ailment.

Nemi Chand Gandhi is a young man of twenty-four. Slight, sallow-complexioned and sporting a wispy beard. He is well dressed in expensive silks and wears two necklaces, of which one is strung with marble-sized beads of beaten gold. He is a Rajasthani domiciled in Hyderabad, a Jain turned worshipper of Goddess Durga, a student politician turned sadhu. I asked him how he had come to acquire siddhi. 'I don't know,' he replied modestly. 'It is the gift of Shakti Ma. I practise what she has given me.' He too has the power to look into the future and has apparently foretold rail accidents and the fall of the Bihar government. I asked him why he had turned his back on politics. 'The whole thing began to disgust me and I renounced the world.' He did not take a guru, believing in the adage: Tu chal akela, ap hi guru ap hi chela (You are both master and student).

Nemi Chand Gandhi is now Chandra Swamy. He travels all over India and Nepal. He has no ashram but spends a lot of time with Andhra peasants. During the nine days of Navratri, he goes into samadhi neither eating nor drinking. 'Whatever I gain during those nine days sustains me for the remaining 356 days of the year.' He went on to explain his philosophy: 'The world can take dukha (pain and adversity), it is sukha (success) that people cannot digest.'

The third encounter is with Dadaji who comes like a breath of fresh air. He displays occult powers which he disowns. He is a 'Godman' but vehemently denounces the cult of gurus and godmen by condemning them as charlatans who are misleading humanity. 'Expose them!' he exhorted me. 'And if you can't do that, get them together through an invitation and let me disprove their pretensions.'

When I called on him at the house of actor Abhi Bhattacharya, he placed his hand on my shoulders and made a tingling sensation run through my spine; my body exuded the aroma of a thousand joss sticks. Then, in front of everyone, he plucked a wristwatch out of my chest. It was a Seiko made in Japan. Everyone examined it. Once on my wrist he ran the palm of his hand over it and asked me to look at it again. The word Seiko vanished. Instead it bore my name (misspelt) and the name of the donor, Dadaji. He knew my weakness for whisky. Out of nowhere appeared a bottle of Scotch, the like of which I have never seen. A white porcelain flask entitled 'Dreamland Whisky, Made in the Universe', with my name printed at its base. Then a blank paper held in my hand was as suddenly covered with a message in red ink from Sri Sri Satyanarayana.

I am baffled.

(1973)

THE GITA AND THE AGNOSTIC

'Religion is based, I think, primarily and mainly, upon fear. It is partly the terror of the unknown and partly the wish to feel that you have a kind of elder brother who will stand by you in all your troubles and disputes. Fear is the basis of the whole thing—fear of the mysterious, fear of defeat, fear of death,' wrote Bertrand Russell in his *Why I Am Not a Christian*. I am in complete agreement with Russell. Like him, although I indulge in religious music and literature, I do not accept the basic statements of religion. But unlike Russell I believe in tradition and the sense of belonging that comes with observance of external symbols—e.g. unshorn hair and beard for a Sikh. Also I feel both the man of religion who says there is a God and the atheist who says there is not are equally presumptuous; I prefer the humbler agnostic attitude: 'I don't know.'

The Gita is one of my favourite pieces of religious literature (the Old Testament and the latter portions of the Quran are the other two). Let me tell you why, though an agnostic, I value the Gita. It is the most important work on Hindu religion, the culmination of the teaching of the Vedas and the Upanishads, 'the most exalted of India's religious poems' (Basham)—the Bible of modern Hinduism. Its influence on the Hindu mind, particularly on the minds of the sophisticated, is incalculable. It is the mainspring of the renaissance of Hinduism today—evidenced by the proliferation all over the country of Gita Pracharini Sabhas.

Gandhiji acknowledged it as his spiritual reference book. He wrote: 'When doubts haunt me, when disappointments stare me in the face, and I see not one ray of hope on the horizon, I turn to the Bhagavad Gita and find a verse to comfort me; and I immediately begin to smile in the midst of overwhelming sorrow.'

The Gita has inspired much religious and secular writing. Its echoes can be heard in the songs of the Sikh Gurus—notably in the haunting melancholy of the compositions of the ninth Guru, Tegh

Bahadur. Its spirit is summarized in Kipling's famous poem 'If' and it was the basis of Aldous Huxley's *The Perennial Philosophy*.

We are still not sure when exactly the Gita was composed. But from the fact that it has no reference to Buddhism, it can be presumed it is pre-Buddhist. Its Sanskrit is also of the style of the older passages of the Mahabharata. Scholars, therefore, believe it must have been written about 500 BCE. Its legendary author is said to have been the sage Vyasa.

We are not quite sure why the Gita has been incorporated in the Mahabharata. Nor of the symbolism (if indeed there is any symbolism at all) in the fact that the Mahabharata consists of eighteen books, the Gita has eighteen chapters and the battle of Kurukshetra lasted eighteen days. It is likely that this philosophical work was put inside a popular epic to ensure its readership, to give the philosophic kernel a sugar-coating to make it palatable. It is often described as the inner shrine of the vast temple of the Mahabharata.

Let me also spell out my personal interpretation of the Gita. It opens with the blind king Dhritarashtra's charioteer, Sanjaya, offering to restore Dhritarashtra's sight so he can watch the spectacle. The grief-stricken king replies: 'If it is to see my sons and nephews and kinsmen engaged in destroying each other that you will restore light to my eyes, then I would rather stay blind.'

A similar grief weighs down the heart of the Pandava Arjuna. 'War even against evil is wrong,' thinks Arjuna. 'It is wrong because it leads to the destruction of the family which in turn has calamitous consequences on society. Why fight for earthly gains?' he asks.

It is apparent that Kurukshetra is symbolic of the battle of life. Arjuna, the personification of the thinking man, is concerned with the ultimate values; his doubts are the doubts of any thinking man who ponders such problems and is involved in the search for truth.

Krishna is the guide, philosopher and friend who provides the answers. The allegory of the chariot, the charioteer and the passenger alluded to in the Upanishads is no mere coincidence; it is used for the same striving of the human soul towards the ultimate.

The sermon of the Bhagavad Gita thus opens with Arjuna's dilemma. He is convinced that his cause is just and the battle he is about to engage in is a dharmayuddha—the battle for the sake of righteousness. Yet he cannot bring himself to kill his own brethren. He is dejected, lets the bow fall from his hand and says firmly: 'I will not fight.' Knowing that it is treason for a commander to make such a statement on the eve of battle. But he is willing to face the consequences of treasonous inaction and defeat rather than soil his hands with the blood of his kinsmen.

Krishna, his charioteer-mentor, answers that only God can take life (which he has also given)—man is only an instrument of his inscrutable design. 'He who thinks he slays, he who thinks he is slain, fails to perceive the truth that he neither slays nor is slain'. As a matter of fact, says Krishna, 'there is no death in the sense of a final dissolution because the eternal in man cannot die, it is only a passing from one form to another. Just as a person casts off worn-out clothes and dons new ones, so man when he shakes off this mortal coil is reborn in some other form. For one that is born, death is certain; for one who dies birth is certain,' assures Krishna and concludes that a man should perform his duty regardless of consequences. 'In the hour of trial,' says Krishna, 'strong men should not despair because then they will lose both heaven and earth. They should arise like a fire that burns all before it.'

For a soldier it is to go to battle when the call to battle comes. All human beings are in a sense soldiers in the battle of life and must likewise perform duties allotted to them. But the performance of this duty should be without consideration for reward—nishkama karma. Says Krishna: 'Treating alike pleasure and pain, gain and loss, victory and defeat...then go to battle.'

The same principle holds good in everyday life–to perform tasks allotted to us should be our only right and privilege—never the fruits of our endeavour.' (One will recall the words scribbled by Robert Falcon Scott, the Antarctic explorer, in his diary as he lay down to die: 'It is the effort that counts, not the applause that follows.')

How can a mortal achieve this state of mental equilibrium in which pleasure and pain, gain and loss, victory and defeat are equally inconsequential? How can one undertake a task with the sole object of performing a duty without craving the returns? Arjuna asks Krishna:

'Describe a man who is so wise, so steadfast in the performance of his duty. How does he speak, sit, sleep and wake? How do we recognize him?'

Krishna replies: 'When a man puts away all desires out of his mind, when his spirit is content in itself, then he becomes stable in intelligence. He should draw away the sense from the object of the sense as a turtle draws its head and legs into its shell. If, on the other hand, a person dwells on the objects of the sense, he inevitably gets attached to those objects. Attachment leads to desire; desire when frustrated leads to anger, anger to bewilderment, bewilderment to loss of memory, loss of memory to destruction of intelligence—and so does man perish. Those whom the gods wish to destroy, they first make mad.

'He into whom desires enter as waters into the sea which though ever being fed by rivers is not agitated, attains peace. It is a kind of peace which passeth understanding. It is tantamount to attaining salvation in one's lifetime and becoming a jivanmukta.'

'How does one attain jivanmukti?'

'There are different ways depending on a person's constitution, temperament, inclination and personality. There is the way of knowledge (jnana marga) for men of contemplation; there is the way of action (karma marga) for men of action; and there is the way of love and devotion (bhakti marga).'

'That may well be so,' interposes Arjuna as he thinks of other things. 'So often in the world does wrong triumph over right, so often good men suffer while evil men live long, healthy and happy lives. If there be no reward for good, no punishment for evil, why should one bother very much?'

Krishna replies: 'Whenever righteousness declines and evil is in the ascendant, I am reborn, reincarnated as the Avatar (redeemer) to protect the good and destroy evildoers, to re-establish dharma (the law). So do I come into this world from age to age. Do not, therefore, worry unduly on this matter as right must ultimately and inevitably triumph over wrong. Satyameva Jayate—because I am God, the righter of wrongs, the sustainer of eternal law, dharma. All I ask of you human beings is that you do your duty in the spirit of renunciation.'

'Renunciation?' queries Arjuna. 'Is giving up everything one has in the world renunciation?'

'No, not that,' replies Krishna. 'It is the unselfish performance of the allotted task, performance of duty in the spirit of renunciation which can only be acquired by the practice of yoga.'

Krishna then explains yoga as the shutting out of all external objects, fixing the inner vision between the eyebrows, controlling the breath and making the mind so one-pointed as to become oblivious of all desires, anxieties and irritations.

In this state of transcendental meditation you will realize that the source of all evil is the ego—ahamkara (I making). But this ego can also be the mainspring of salvation. A man must redeem himself by himself, for self alone is the lord of self, self the only means of salvation—'atta hi attano natho, atta hi attano gati.'

Krishna then tells Arjuna the essentials of yogic meditation. The need for physical well-being (yoga is not for those who eat too much or too little, or sleep too much or too little)—one has to live a temperate and well-regulated life, seek a quiet place, sit cross-legged on a deerskin and make the mind one-pointed. The state of one who does achieve this is 'like a lamp in a windless place which flickers not'. To such a one comes the knowledge that God is omniscient, omnipresent, omnipotent—and in the heart of all of us.

'I am the ritual and the sacrifice...the sacred hymn and the offering,' says Krishna. 'I am seated in the hearts of all creatures; I am the beginning, the middle and the end. Amongst gods I am Vishnu, among lights I am the sun'—and so on.

'I am God, I accept all worship as equally valid,' assures Krishna. 'Whatever form of worship a devotee performs, I make his faith steady... whosoever offers me with devotion a leaf, a flower, a fruit or water, that offering of love from the pure of heart I accept.'

This sentiment is beautifully echoed in a Tamil folk song:

Into the bosom of the one great sea
Flow streams that come from hills on every side
Their names are various as their springs
And thus in every land do men bow down

To one great God, though known by many names.
The great-souled, O Partha, who abide in the divine nature,
knowing (me as) the imperishable source of all beings,
worship me with an undistracted mind.
Always glorifying me, strenuous and steadfast in vows,
bowing down to me with devotion, they worship me,
ever disciplined.

(1971)

LOVING IS GIVING

'Let me tell you of a fable which illustrates the character of our society today,' he said in his soft, gurgling voice. 'There were two men who were close friends. One was blind, the other lame. They helped each other; the blind man took the lame man on his shoulders, the lame man showed the blind one the way. So the friendship was good for both of them. Then they fell out. And as often happens when close friends fall out, they became the bitterest of enemies. One day God sent for the lame man and asked him to ask for a boon. Instead of begging for his legs to be restored, the lame man said: 'O God, please deprive that blind fellow of his legs.' God then sent for the blind man and likewise asked him to ask for whatever he wanted. The blind man replied: 'Please God, take the light out of the eyes of that lame chap.'

This simple parable was narrated by Swami Muktanandaji in his sylvan ashram at Ganeshpuri. Why he had chosen to use this parable became clear to me as I watched the crowd, consisting largely of foreign disciples, participating in the function organized to give 360 Adivasi families kitchen utensils and saris. 'Where does all this money come from?' some Indian critics had been asking.

A good bit of it comes from foreigners who come to seek solace and peace in the ashram. The more important question, 'Where does all this money go?' is seldom asked. The answer is easily available. Drive beyond Santa Cruz airport into the densely forested hillside inhabited by the Adivasis of Thana district and see for yourself. All along the route up to the temple of Vajreshwari and beyond have gone up grey cement pucca dwellings gifted by the Muktananda Trust to homeless Adivasis. Thirty-five lakh rupees have been spent on this laudable enterprise. The aim is to put a solid roof over every Adivasi family in the entire district. This makes sense even to an agnostic allergic to godmen. So does Baba (as Swamiji is referred to) when he says, 'God dwells within each one of you, the only way to see him in others is to love them.'

Baba is a rare phenomenon among the godmen of today. He is no Dilip Kumar, he is garishly dressed in a comical woollen cap, dark glasses, saffron robes and ghastly pink socks. And yet he has a charisma which captivates all who come near him. At the meeting I went to, there were men and women from thirty-seven nations and of all faiths (Hindus, Muslims, Christians) and races (Caucasians, Blacks, Arabs and Jews). Baba draws them like a piece of crystal sugar draws flies.

(1977)

THE MESSAGE OF GURU NANAK

The Sikhs are celebrating the 500th birthday of the founder of their faith. For the last ten years they have been planning for these celebrations—to raise new universities, colleges, hospitals and schools; publish literature; arrange seminars and lectures; organize the non-stop chanting of hymns; take out massive processions; entertain their friends at tea parties and banquets. Some of these schemes have been carried out, many will remain unfulfilled. And almost everyone will feel that much more could have been achieved if only... The chief cause of Sikh frustration comes from the feeling that the message of Nanak was not really conveyed to non-Sikhs and that the participation of other communities was merely symbolic, a gesture of goodwill. No more.

The sense of frustration is inevitable. People are not really interested in faiths and practices other than their own. It is also an error to believe that processions, meetings, lectures and literature influence people's minds. They have little or no impact. It is not the excellence of the life of a prophet or his teaching that matters (lives of prophets as well as their messages have a quality of sameness); what matters is the way of life and conduct of those that profess to be his followers. In the final analysis Guru Nanak will be judged not by what he did and said but by what his followers today do, say, and the way they behave towards other people.

There is an element of simplicity in Nanak's life and teachings. His life was an example of Thomas Paine's precepts: 'The world is my country, all mankind are my brethren, and to do good is my religion.' His teachings could be summed up in two words—works and worship—in that order. Only he put it all in very beautiful poetry. If the Sikhs really wish to pay homage to their founder-Guru and impress their non-Sikh friends with his greatness, they have an excellent opportunity to do so. We are the world's poorest country with the highest proportion of non-workers—beggars, sadhus, yogis. This places a bigger burden on those who, like the Sikhs, believe in the adage

'Work is worship'. Work harder so that there is something to spare for the needy. Also in recent years the atmosphere in our country has been fouled by communal passions. Nanak made the bringing of Hindus and Muslims together the chief mission of his life. What greater way is there to do honour to his memory than by continuing that crusade? Sikhs could play a unique role in organizing corps of volunteers in our towns and villages dedicated to the task of keeping the peace, of fostering fraternal relations between communities and by making their gurdwaras sanctuaries for victims of communal frenzy. Nanak became the king of holy men (Shah fakir) because the Hindus recognized him as their Guru, the Mussalmans as their pir. Nanak's Sikhs could emulate his example. Let me coin a doggerel for them:

Singh Soorma Shah Sardar Hindu ka dost, Mussulman ka yaar.

(Undated)

FINIS TO RIOTING

A few weeks ago there were communal riots in some parts of the country. I met one of the victims—a handsome youth, educated abroad and, like many anglicized young men, totally oblivious of whether he was Hindu or Muslim. He sported a deep gash on one arm. He told me of the incident. He had heard of the riot in the town but had ignored it as something that happened between Hindus and Muslims—he was neither because he only thought of himself as an Indian. He had finished his day's work and was on his way home in a friend's car. Suddenly they came up against a solid phalanx of men armed with lathis and crowbars. The friend tried to turn back as fast as he could. The men were faster. 'A bunch of armed goondas can be a terrifying spectacle,' he explained. 'They pelted the car with stones and began to smash it with their lathis. I realized they were after me. I did not want my friend to suffer because of me. I jumped out of the car and tried to bolt. I stumbled and fell. A volley of lathis came crashing on my head. I got up and ran. I outdistanced my pursuers but other armed men from side streets joined in the chase. I was exhausted. I stopped and decided to die like a man. Just then my friend ran up and shielded me. Three other men linked their arms and made a chain to guard me. "You will not touch him till you have killed us," they declared. It was a miracle. Four men facing an armed mob of four hundred! And they won. The mob dispersed. And here I am to tell the tale.' There was no bitterness in his voice. He summed up the nightmarish experience in simple, telling words and a wistful smile. 'Till that evening all I knew about myself was that I was an Indian; it took a few lathi blows to pierce my skull and make me understand that I am a Muslim.' I asked him if he had any views on how communal riots could be prevented. He replied: 'My experience proves that it takes one man of courage to defy a hundred armed goondas. The rioter is a coward ashamed of what he is up to, wanting an excuse to give it up. The other thing is speed. If the police get into action at once, tension can be defused without much difficulty. But if they waste time securing permission from magistrates to disperse mobs and make arrests, etc., they only add to their troubles.' I am convinced that the government can write finis to the sordid chapter on communal rioting by introducing a riot code giving the police the right to shoot, arrest, publicly flog miscreants and impose collective fines on localities where incidents take place. All patriotic Indians will support the measure.

(1972)

DADAJI—THE MAN OF MIRACLES

I have no faith. I've never felt the need for it. Faith is denial of reason and for me reason is supreme. But I do not question the right of people to stick to their faiths because I have seen the good that it can do to some of them. I do not believe in miracles any more than I do in magic. But I do not deny that there are phenomena which still baffle scientists. I say this as a prelude to narrating my encounter with Amiya Roy Chowdhury, known to his innumerable admirers as Dadaji.

I received two books on Dadaji. They were compilations of tributes by eminent doctors, professors and businessmen, all of whom had experienced some miracle or the other. My interest was roused.

A few days later, film star Abhi Bhattacharya breezed into my office to take me to meet Dadaji. The happy glow on his handsome face made me suspect that he had already counted me amongst his dharma bhais.

I report the encounter without any prejudice or bias.

The reception room in Dadaji's apartment in Bandra had no furniture except a divan which was obviously meant for Dadaji. At the time there were only half a dozen men and women, all Bengalis. Then Dadaji entered. Everyone stood up. One man prostrated himself, placing his head on Dadaji's feet.

Dadaji is tall and light-skinned. He wears his black hair long. His youthful handsomeness belies his seventy years. His eyes have a hypnotic spell-binding power. An aroma known in esoteric circles as the padmagandha (fragrance of the lotus) fills the room.

Dadaji seats himself on the divan and beckons to me. I shuffle up and sit near his feet. He tries to fix me in a kindly but hypnotic stare. He wants to know why I have come to see him. I tell him of my lack of faith, my disbelief in the existence of a divine power and my curiosity about him and his following.

'What if Sri Satya Narayan wants to communicate with you?' he asks. I look puzzled. 'What if he sends you a memento?' he asks again. He raises his right hand in the air, and in his palm appears a medallion with an image of an elderly man. 'It is Sri Satya Narayan's gift to you,' assures Dadaji. 'No, it is not,' I protest. 'You, Dadaji, have given it to me.' He smiles. 'I am no one, it is all the doing of Sri Satya Narayan.

'What is your name?' he asks. I tell him. He takes back the medallion, rubs the reverse side with his thumb. What had been a blank surface is now embossed with my name. Only my name is not correctly spelt. A minute later and as mysteriously as before a gold chain appears in the palm of his empty hand. 'This is to wear the medallion around your neck,' he says giving it to me.

'Come with me,' orders Dadaji. I follow him. He leads me into his bedroom.

Once more we are on different levels; he sits on his bed, I on the floor beside him. He tells me he is a monist. Sri Satya Narayan pervades the entire universe. There are no gurus. Each man is his own guru because he is a part of Sri Satya Narayan. The way to salvation is through Mahanam (the great name). It can be in any language.

'You ask for it in your own mother tongue.' He hands me a blank slip of paper and asks me to bow before a picture of Sri Satya Narayan. I do so. The paper now bears two words in Gurmukhi, 'Gopal, Govinda.' A minute later the paper is blank again. Apparently the message has been delivered and does not need to be on paper any more. And so it continues. A touch of his hand on my beard fills my beard with the same padmagandha.

For an unbeliever it is a traumatic kind of experience. It does not shake my disbelief in religion or miracles nor bends my reason to accept banal statements about God, Guru and the Name which pass for philosophy in our land. But let the reader make up his own mind.

(1972)

THE NATURAL WORLD

SHIVALIK MONKEYS

In late September and early October, not a flower is to be seen on the hillsides. Not many birds, and little bird song. All day long, I sit in the garden looking at the deep blue sky and an occasional white cloud floating lazily whichever way the winds take it. My garden, normally full of the chattering of white-cheeked bulbuls and cawing of crows, is strangely silent. In the afternoon a troop of langurs arrives from nowhere and begins stripping leaves off fruit trees. A large mama langur carrying her little baby perches herself on my birdbath to drink water. She ducks her baby's head down to teach it how to drink. A male langur strolls across the lawn and seats himself majestically on the bench, watching his family from where he sits. Another plants himself on the tank a couple of yards away and glares at me through his malevolent yellow eyes as if asking why I am where I am. Another cheeky fellow seats himself on a branch of the toon tree under which I sit. His long tail dangles a couple of feet above my head. There are a dozen of them chasing each other on the corrugated tin roof, romping about the lawn, completely at home in my home. They make me feel like a trespasser on their domain. They seem to have driven rhesus monkeys away from my side of Kasauli. I haven't seen a rhesus in the two days I have been here and never before have so many langurs invaded my property. They are beautiful animals, silver-grey, jet-black faces, sinuous bodies and long tails. And not as aggressive as the rhesus. Why the rhesus is scared of them, I do not know.

The one thing I have against langurs (and the rhesus) is that they have taken to chewing telephone wires. My telephone was dead for two days till the wires were replaced. I hope the wire is coated with stuff that monkeys don't relish.

(2001)

MATING SEASON

It begins in spring when young people's thoughts turn to love. Nature renews itself. Withered leaves fall, new ones take their place. Animals and birds pair up to mate. Their metabolism specifies when females come into heat and become receptive to the advances of the male of their species. The only exceptions are humans. They remain on heat round the year: for them all seasons are mating seasons.

By the time spring turns to summer, birds have prepared their nests to lay eggs. Females of the animal species are pregnant and ready to deliver as soon as nature is ready to provide them sustenance. Come the monsoon and the parched land turns green. Trees bear fruit. Insects multiply by the millions to assure adequate food for birds and their hatchlings. Rains renew life by providing food for all living creatures.

I see this process of regeneration around my little apartment. Some years ago my neighbours drove away dozens of cats that had made my home their own. They said cats spread disease. This was at the height of the bubonic plague epidemic in Surat. My cats were removed to a cats' home. They never came back. A couple of months ago two strays decided to move into my backyard. They refused to befriend me. Then one of them had a litter of three kittens behind a bush. I tried to make friends with the kittens. Every time I saw them playing on the patch of green, I approached them with friendly noises. They simply glowered at me with their large questioning eyes. If I took a step forward, they disappeared behind the bushes.

But there was my granddaughter's cat, Billo, who spent a lot of her time purring in my lap when no one else was around. We looked forward to her having a litter because she was often missing from the home and evidently cohabiting with a tom who prowled around in the backyard. At times Billo's belly looked swollen. We surmised she was pregnant. Then just as suddenly the swelling disappeared. It was probably a false pregnancy—or just surplus gas.

However, I did notice that she frequently visited the linen cupboard at the farthest end of my flat. It was in the lowest shelf of this cupboard that most cats I'd had gave birth to their litter. Then one day without warning Billo hid herself in the linen cupboard and emerged after an hour or so mewing incessantly. She wanted to draw my attention to something. She led me to the linen cupboard. I peered inside. I could not see anything but distinctly heard a tiny mew. We celebrated the arrival of Billo's progeny. I still do not know if it is just one, or as is usual with cats, two or three. I look forward to having them play in my lap. There are few other things as endearing as kittens at play.

During the mating season in the animal world, sex is compulsive. That poses a problem for humans who are particular about the pedigrees of their pets. They take great pains to keep their pedigreed bitches from mating with aira-ghaira animals till they have found an equally high-pedigreed mate for them.

One such person is my friend Claire Dutt who keeps three Labradors. Two are now past breeding, only one, Zoe, is still of the age to breed and Claire is on the lookout for a suitable match for her. She sends her dogs out for an airing in the park with her servant. Apparently she sensed that while her servant was enjoying his bidi, Zoe had been up to no good with some stray dog. She was understandably upset and questioned her servant about it. His reply was charmingly naive: 'Memsahib, the two old dogs behave very well but this Zoe—iska chaal challan kharaab ho gayaa hai—whenever she meets a male dog, she says hello, hello, hello to him.'

(2002)

FLAMING TREES

There was a time when just before Holi I used to drive round the Ridge and go to Surajkund just to see the flame of the forest in bloom. This otherwise nondescript, small-sized tree came into its full glory only for a brief week but it was a sight for the gods. It has several Indian names like palas, dhaak, and tessoo and is found across the length and breadth of our country. Its beetle-black buds contrast with the bright and curving petals which resemble a parrot's beak—and give it a spectacular look. It is not commonly known that the Battle of Plassey (1757) came to be so named because it was fought on a field that had lots of palas trees in bloom at the time.

I do not drive out anymore and am content to see an imitation of palas in coral trees which grow in some of our parks—their petals are of the same colour as that of the palas but are not curved. Neither flower has any fragrance. Now I sit in my nature-perfumed garden among colourful cineraria, salvias and ixora. Some years ago, I planted what I was assured was a kadam. It grew very rapidly to a great height and has thick large-leaved foliage. It has become the favourite of a variety of birds, including green barbets which call all day long. It gets pale flowers which have no odour. It is not a kadam, what it is no one has yet been able to tell me. At Holi time it begins to shed its leaves. The slightest whiff of air and they come on my head and all around me like confetti showered on a newly married couple. My gardener sweeps them up twice a day but for a week the pat-jhar (leaf-shedding) continues unabated till the tree is stripped bare. And suddenly new fiery-red leaves appear which gradually turn to green. Within a few days, the tree is thick with leaves as before and a safe haven for birds.

I am closer to nature in my little garden than driving around parks and gardens. There is a noticeable drop in the number of sparrows these days. And while we are coming to the end of March and mango trees are in flower, I have yet to hear the koel which by now should have regained its full-throated cry—'koo-oo, koo-oo'. What's happened to them?

Though all too brief, this is the pleasantest time of the year in northern India. Whichever way you turn, there are flowers; whenever you pause to listen there is bird song. Meer Taqi Meer caught the atmosphere of spring time in a few memorable lines:

If you like to visit the garden, go now;
For this is the month of spring;
The leaves are green and flowering trees
Are in full bloom;
The clouds hang low
And rain is gently falling
The heart feels like a throbbing wound,
The tears have turned to one red flood
This crimson-faced poppy of love
Dries up life and drains all blood
This is the time when fresh, green leaves
Appear upon the trees;
And branch and twig of plant and shrub
Are bent with bloom and seed
With blaze of roses' colour, Meer,
The garden is on fire;
The bulbul sounds a warning note:
Go past, O Sir, beware!

(2003)

SPRINGTIME

Spring is the time to go and look at our countryside. I don't mean the false spring of Basant day though, according to an old saying, with the arrival of Basant, the cold weather takes wing and flies away. For here up north where the cold is real and the winds blow in earnest, the festival of spring with all its bright yellow turbans and gay mustard coloured dupattas can make you shiver and seek the warmth and comfort of the fireside at home.

I remember the 5th of February this year when a steady north wind brought down a taste of the high Himalayas. Looking windward, we caught a glimpse of snow-covered peaks beyond a gap in the wintry blue of the foothills. There was no yellow in the fields beyond the new township, the infant wheat plants were of a dull green colour, the gram was no more than an untidy eruption clinging to the hard surface of the earth. There was perhaps a sense of vigour in the air, a feeling that a tremendous effort was somewhere taking place, and as I walked through the fields I was enveloped by a strong wintry aroma—a glorious health-giving mixture of smells which rose from brown grass, young green fields, the plants of rape and mustard, cow dung cakes baking dry in the sun and the smoke of village fires. But the gaiety, the joy and abandon of fulfilment had yet to come.

And they have come now that March has brought the real spring to us. The wheat is now waist-high and the bearded ears heavy with the burden of fat grains which sway with a drunken rhythm as a light breeze touches them. A gentle ripple starts at one end of the field and goes whispering all the way to the other side. The wheat fields are a bright rich green, the sort of green Gauguin liked to lay on his canvas straight from the tube. The gram plants are a deeper and duller green but they are dotted with little pink and mauve flowers. The sarson is in full bloom and as you pass by the gaiety of the yellow flowers shining in the morning sun takes possession of you. You stop and inhale the pungent flavour of the air at this spot. The fields are hedged off with dry thorn bushes and men and cattle walk along narrow dust-tracks that wind their picturesque way from one village to another.

How many of you who live in towns and make plans and blueprints talk of the rural wealth of India and the uplift of villagers have seen and felt the overpowering beauty of our countryside in spring? It is only when you begin to feel a constriction in your throat and your eyes begin to smart that you will know how important rural India is spiritually even more than materially.

(1957)

THE LIFE AROUND US

During a visit to a school in a northern state I was very pleasantly surprised to see a class of six or seven boys deeply absorbed in pasting leaves in their albums. There is little emphasis on nature study in our educational system, so this extracurricular activity attracted my attention.

'What is this thing you are putting in your album?' I asked one of the boys.

'A leaf.'

'Leaf of what?'

'A tree, of course! What else can it be?'

All the boys sniggered at my silly questions and resumed their leaf-pressing without any doubts on the futility of the pastime. Their teacher was not so embarrassed as I expected. He later confessed to me that he did not know the names of more than a dozen trees himself.

'What is the use of learning the names of trees and birds?' he said aggressively. 'Our new principal has just returned from England and he wants us to do the sort of things they do there.'

It is true that interest in natural life is found more among English people than any others. Interest in birds is spoken of as snobisme anglais (English snobbery) by the French. But that is no reason for indifference to the life about us. Our vast variety of birds, animals and trees is amongst our richest treasures and yet most of us know very little about them. This is very surprising because as a nation we are friendlier towards birds and beasts than any other people in the world. Here sparrows nest in our cooking vessels, mynas walk in and out between our feet and monkeys clamber into railway compartments at wayside stations… And yet if you ask even an educated Indian how many birds or plants he can recognize, his list will not go beyond a dozen. 'I am not an ornithologist or a botanist,' he will say smugly.

There is no particular merit in simply knowing the names of trees or birds: a rose by any other name will smell as sweet. Nevertheless, it seems silly not to know a rose as a rose, or in our context to wax lyrical about the bulbul without knowing what it looks like or how unmusical it can be, or recite verses about the papeeha and not know when it cries its head off in the mango grove.

This is not all there is to knowing a name. It may be the first step in knowing to what uses something can be put. An amusing anecdote is told about the first French Ambassador to Nepal. When he was driving up to the palace to present his credentials, he noticed whole hillsides of artichokes in flower. He made a last minute change in his address, adding that he was delighted to see that the Nepalese and Frenchmen shared one pleasure in common—the love of eating artichokes.

That was the first time that people in Kathmandu heard that artichokes could be eaten, up till then they had looked upon it as a noxious weed.

(1957)

KILLER TURNS LOVER

One summer afternoon I cycled out of the city with a gun strapped to my shoulder. It was the breeding season for birds and shooting was forbidden. That was good enough reason to want to shoot.

For several hours I trudged through the hot and dusty countryside and saw nothing except crows and mynas. In sheer exasperation I shot a crow sleeping on a keekar tree. The entire crow population of the neighbourhood filled the sky with their protesting cries. I shot another two on the wing to frighten them off. I left the three birds gasping and bleeding on the ground. 'No use wasting eight anna shots on dying crows,' I said to myself, 'the jackals will finish them off at night.'

The way back home was along a canal bank. Round the bend I suddenly came across a partridge with a brood of six or seven chicks. She spread out her wings and hurried them off under a nearby bush. I got off my bicycle and loaded my gun. I threw stones into the bush. The chicks were not used to human beings and came scuttling out. Their mother could not remain hidden and followed them. She tried to lead me away by pretending she was injured and could be caught. She let one of her wings hang on the ground as if it was broken. I look quick aim and fired. The hen collapsed in a cloud of feathers. The chicks scattered away in terror. I put the partridge triumphantly in my bag and rode home.

I had left three birds fluttering on a dusty field and a brood of six baby partridges barely two days old to fend for themselves.

That night I could not sleep.

◆

The birds in the house knew I was a killer and flew off as soon as they saw me, they did so even if I did not carry a gun or a catapult. At first I was peeved and angry. Then I realized why they fled from me and decided to make friends with them. It took a long time to win their confidence. This is how it happened.

The window of the office where I worked was framed by a thick creeper. A pair of bulbuls built their nest in it. When I discovered it, there were three eggs in it. The bulbuls were alarmed at my discovery and spent the whole afternoon quarrelling with each other. The agitated chirping was as clear to me as human speech. 'Chuk chuk chuk,' nagged the hen. 'Didn't I tell you not to make the nest so near that nasty man?' 'Chuk chuk chuk,' replied the male. 'If you knew about him why did you lay your eggs here?'

For the next two days I did not hear a cheep; only the sound of flapping wings told me of their coming and going as they stood guard over the eggs. On the third day the argument started again. 'So very much like married couples,' I said to myself. But surely I had done nothing to excite their suspicion? I tiptoed to the window to see what was amiss. It was a great relief to discover that it wasn't me they were running down; it was a tomcat who had discovered their nest and was sitting a few feet away with its eyes glued on it. I shooed away the tomcat and the birds were quiet once more.

Thereafter I had to come to the rescue of the bulbuls several times. Each time the tomcat came that way they set up an agitated 'chuk chuk chuk.' I had a pile of stones on my worktable which I learnt to use with deadly accuracy on the cat. When the eggs hatched, I had to increase my vigilance and practically share the upbringing of the nestlings with the bulbuls. The battle between me and the cat was waged round the clock. I shifted my bed to the office.

Then one day I found the nest empty. Had the bulbuls taken their young to safety or had the tomcat done its devilish job? I threw the pile of stones on the table into the waste paper basket and tried to get down to some work. I heard the 'chuk chuk chuk' at a distance. It must be my imagination, I said to myself, and went on with my work. Then the 'chuk chuk' came nearer. Finally, the two bulbuls flew into the office, and around my head, calling in the most agitated manner. 'Hurry, hurry,' said one alighting on my notebook, 'and stop this pen pushing.' I got up and went out. The three nestlings were perched on a branch of a tree. A couple of feet below them sat the tomcat patiently waiting for them to fall off. I picked up a stone and hurled it with all the venom I had. It hit the tomcat above his tail and he fled with a loud 'Miaow.'

I do not know whether birds have a language. They certainly communicate with each other.

Word got around that I was no longer the nasty man who killed birds. I had actually saved the bulbul children's lives. Birds no longer flew away when they saw me. Some even made friends with me. The magpie robin often came to my window and gave a free performance of ballet dancing and singing which would make Balasaraswati and Subbulakshmi turn green with envy.

◆

My interest in birds has changed from curiosity to affection. I can recommend it as a most satisfying hobby. It rewards you in strange ways. I recall an incident a few years ago. It was a torridly hot day in June—not a cloud in the grey sky, not a breath of wind to stir the limp, dust-laden leaves. And an interminable meeting of civil servants with the boss droning away like a bumblebee. I heard a bird call—a long, anguished wail which only the pied crested cuckoo can produce. I got up from the chair and went to the window. The boss stopped droning and everyone looked up at me as if I had been touched by the summer sun. 'What is the matter?' he asked me angrily. 'It is going to rain tomorrow. That is the monsoon bird calling.' They looked at each other and smiled knowingly. What with the heat and big turban on the head...

Next day at the same time black nimbus clouds spread across the sky and it poured with rain. I was no longer the slightly loony Sikh working in the office but a man who held converse with Nature and understood its mysterious messages spoken by the birds.

(1958)

MASSACRE AS SPORT

In the bad old days of the British Raj, when maharajas were rulers of their principalities and a princely shikar assumed the proportions of a war of extinction waged by man against bird and beast, I succeeded in wangling an invitation to a shoot at Bharatpur. K. P. S. Menon was then diwan of the state; Lord Linlithgow was the chief guest. There were fifty others. We were supplied with maps of the swamps and woodland with our posts marked. We were given cartridges by the bucketful, provided with orderlies who would help to reload our guns and pickers who would retrieve what we brought down. In the early hours we were driven to our butts, which were camouflaged with leaves, and asked to await the signal—the opening shot by the Viceroy.

As the eastern horizon turned grey, we heard the thud of the viceregal gun come over the water. The sky was soon full of millions of birds. Guns opened up in different parts of the battlefield. A few minutes later several flights of birds which I could not identify came towards my hideout. I banged away for all I was worth. There were so many that it was easier to hit than to miss them. By the time the sun was up I had fired over a hundred cartridges. A variety of bloodied waterfowl executed by me lay about my feet. I then saw that I had killed many which were inedible: cormorants, ibises, spoonbills, moorhens, coots. In clearer light I realized that in the massed flights of teal, geese, mallard and pintail it was not easy to separate the edible from the inedible. I also realized that the pellets spread in so wide a radius that for every two or three birds that fell an equal number were injured—to die of festering wounds or become helpless victims of predators.

After a few hours, the bugle was sounded for ceasefire. The guests assembled under a shamiana and were served with iced champagne. What we had killed was laid out for our inspection. The count ran into the thousands. As politeness required, the highest score was attributed to the Viceroy, with His Highness a close second. The rest of us wrangled over our bag while being 'pilawed and champagned'.

It was a sickening business. In one morning we had murdered thousands of innocent birds and maimed many thousand more. It could only be described as wanton massacre. When I asked what would be done to all the birds we had killed, I received vague answers to the effect that they would be sent to hospitals in Bharatpur, Agra or Delhi to be consumed by the inmates. I had little doubt that most of them would just rot and be thrown away.

Shikars on this massive scale do not take place anymore. But the massacre continues unabated. One has only to see the way the countryside about our great cities has been denuded of game. Carloads of shikaris go further and further afield, do their work of destruction and come back loaded with partridge and geese and deer. They kill well beyond the need of their tables—and they call it sport. The diplomatic corps take pride of place in this ghoulish pastime. They import ammunition at cheaper rates and they have means of stocking their kill in a deep freeze.

It must be obvious to everyone that neither the high cost of ammunition nor fees for shooting licences, neither closed seasons nor prohibitions against the killing of rarer species of fowl or beast, neither game sanctuaries nor national parks—nor any other law, rule or regulation—can stop the destruction of our wildlife. In view of past experience it is somewhat naive to hope as our Wildlife Board did at its last meeting—that by choosing the Gir lion as our national animal people will become conscious of the peril it is in. By such fanciful logic all we need to do to ameliorate the wretched condition of our Untouchables is to choose a Harijan girl as Miss India.

Serious situations need bold, often unpopular decisions. If we really mean to save our wildlife from extinction, we must impose a total ban on shikar for a year or more. Prohibit the sale of ammunition and sporting rifles, shotguns and other weapons, forbid grants of game licences—and thus come down with a heavy hand on shooting or trapping. A blanket prohibition would be much easier to enforce than specifying seasons for slaughter or earmarking certain species as protected. The move will also be popular with the general mass of people. All said and done this is the land of Mahavira and Gautama and Gandhi. In the minds of most of us ahimsa is still paramo dharma.

(1969)

SEX MATTERS

OUR BEAUTIFUL EROTICA

I often wonder what kind of society we were when the temples of Khajuraho and Konark were constructed. In those times, as it is today, temples were not only places of worship but also places where people socialized, exchanged gossip, arranged marriages and transacted business. Around them grew bazaars, markets and dwellings. Town life centred around them; worship was only a part of the citizens' preoccupation. It must have been a very liberal society, the like of which did not exist anywhere in the world.

Things changed with the advent of Islam and Christianity in the country. They were puritanical faiths which regarded erotica sinful. Hindus imbibed Islam and Victorian attitudes and became equally censorious about matters concerning sex. Some were ashamed of their ancestors' frank portrayals of sexuality; others tried to explain them away as spiritual exercises. This is nonsense. In most temples that have erotic sculptures there is nothing spiritual or mysterious—all forms of sexual variations, homosexual, lesbian, even intercourse with animals, can be seen. The one thing Khajuraho and Konark have in common is artistic excellence, the sculptures however explicit are extremely beautiful. We don't have to apologize to anyone for having and cherishing them. I have no patience with the new 'morality' which has assumed epidemic proportions in our country. Banning books, destroying paintings, censoring films because they are in conflict with the prevailing religious prejudices are unworthy of our liberal past.

(2001)

THE RIGHT TO GO NUDE

It was more than twenty years ago that I was first exposed to people exposing themselves. This was in Sweden. Literally miles of beach with almost everyone from toddlers to octogenarians with not a stitch of clothing on them. I could not ogle at all the nubile nineteen-year-olds as I would have liked to. I was almost drooling in the mouth when my hosts suggested that we all strip and refresh ourselves in the sea. The drooling stopped, my throat went dry. My Indian inhibitions against self-exposure were too strong to overcome. I couldn't even raise my eyes to take a good look at my hostess and her three college-going daughters. I tried to analyse my nudo-phobia and came to the conclusion that I was more scared of taking off my turban and exposing my long hair than I was of taking off my pants and exposing...you know what. I was even more scared of my natural reactions—of showing obvious pleasure at seeing what I was seeing without having to say so. The visions of that sunny Sunday afternoon near Stockholm has troubled many of my midnights' and my noons' reposes.

Since then I have seen a lot of nudity on the beaches of Hawaii, Côte d'Azur and Sydney. I am an unashamed voyeur and liked it all. I was delighted to learn that stodgy old England is about to legalize stripping. As one might expect of a nation of shopkeepers it is not for the sake of health or for the aesthetic pleasure of seeing beautiful people as God made them, but to make money. The issue has come up before the Brighton City Council dominated by conservatives. It would appear that while the lady members are in favour of shedding clothes, the men have certain reservations. A lady member who also runs a lodging house has proved her bona fides by circulating her own photograph in a topless bikini. The reactions of the other members to this form of canvassing is not known. But a male member who is opposed to the 'flagrant exhibition of mammary glands' has been warned by his wife that if he continues to be obdurate she will release the photograph of him taking a sauna bath in mixed company. She clearly has her eye on the cash register. She says, 'I am not a woman of immoral character. I'm one of the most old-fashioned girls. I do not take the pill or go to bed with men, but I believe in this beach. Let's face the facts—we want European tourists, and we want their money. So let's give them the sort of facilities they're used to.'

The lady may be getting far more than she is bargaining for. But even the stodgiest of the councillors concedes that she may have a point. He admits that sometime ago when he chanced upon a couple taking off their clothes he was struck by the beauty of the well-endowed woman and suddenly thought 'that all those years of tedious committees had been worthwhile'.

There may be unexpected pleasures awaiting visitors to Brighton. To wit:

There was a brave damsel of Brighton
Whom nothing could possibly frighten.
She plunged into the sea
And, with infinite glee,
Was taken for a ride by a Triton.

That brings me to the subject of incentives to tourism in India. I dare not suggest that we too go in for nude bathing to attract foreigners, but let us not be too prudish when they wish to expose themselves to our sun, sea, sands and our gazes. Take it from me that nothing will add to the beauty of Calangute or Kovalam more than a shapely teenager streaking across the palm fronds against the setting sun.

(1979)

THE SEXUAL MORALS OF THE RICH AND POWERFUL

Jackie Oh!: An Intimate Biography by Kitty Kelley is indeed intimate! The Prince Charming of America turns out to be the Emperor without clothes in the ancient fable. John Kennedy, the youngest, richest, handsomest president of the United States, had the morals of a randy mountain goat, bestriding any female who came within reach, ranging from the luscious Marilyn Monroe to horsey secretaries, pretty airhostesses and fat barmaids, friends' wives, and mistresses of all ages in all climes. His performance in bed, however, was very perfunctory. A lady press reporter beguiled into a White House bedroom in the belief that she would get a scoop found herself thrown on the bed without as much as an introductory May I? And it was the classical wham, bam, goodbye ma'am. Before the lady realized she was being laid, the President had finished and was zipping up his pants to rejoin his wife and the other guests. We learn that Kennedy was much like a barnyard rooster mounting its harem of clucking hens in rapid succession.

The book, however, is not meant to be about Kennedy but about his wife, Jacqueline. She comes off no better. She is as obsessed with money as her husband was with sex. She is said to have come from the topmost echelons of America's social elite. But her love for the best things of life led her to liaisons with only those who had the means to provide them. As the President's wife she accepted expensive gifts: gold jewellery, diamonds, sapphires, mink, leopard-skin coats. And not long after her husband's assassination she befriended Aristotle Onassis, reported to be the richest man in the world—thirty years older than her and as crude as any guttersnipe of the Athenian slums. (His favourite practical joke was to invite his mistresses to examine his rectum for piles, and when they did so, to fart in their faces.) Jackie made a deal with Onassis. She received millions of dollars for giving him the right to bed her. It makes her the most expensive whore in history.

It is a great pity that the biographer who admittedly was never granted an interview by Jacqueline should nevertheless have gone ahead to collect all the juicy gossip she could and put it together. Although she has succeeded in producing a salaciously readable book, it can scarcely be described as a biography.

(1979)

THE FEMALE BREAST

What is it about a woman that most men fall for? Is it her face or figure? Her eyes or lips? Her bosom, broad hips or her posterior? An anatomical dissection would be futile because it is the totality of her physical makeup (all her body is pasture to mine eyes) plus other intangibles like her temperament and above all her vitality that determine her attractive potential for the male. However, it has also to be conceded that when it comes to what is vulgarly known as sex appeal it is the bosom, the middle or the buttocks that rouse the male libido. Of these three items the pornographer and the voyeur will vote for the pudenda or the rear; the aesthete be he poet, painter or a man of letters will vote for the bosom. No part of the female anatomy has been more exploited by artists and photographers nor more written about by novelists. But it had never occurred to me that there was enough material to devote an entire book to the subject. Alan Brien has achieved that distinction with his *Domes of Fortune*. If our Customs chaps do not ban the book for obscenity and you can afford the rupee equivalent of the dollar price you may be able to read 6,000 words of eulogy and ogle at pictures of bosoms of various shapes and sizes.

Alan Brien has long been my favourite journalist-author. Ever since I ceased getting the *Times* group of papers, including the *Sunday Times,* the two items I have missed most are the crossword puzzle and Alan Brien. I was glad to learn that he has been profitably engaged in field work on the female breast or what in scientific terminology is known as mammarology. Apparently his wife, Jill Tweedie, approved of the project. 'I have never attacked soft porn,' retorted Jill to the insinuation that the two were separating after her husband's 'boobing' for the sake of money. 'The interesting thing about breasts is that they change all the time,' writes Alan Brien. When a woman is running, or angry, or wearing a sweater, a breast is the most restless thing in the world. But when it comes to penning variations to the theme, Alan does not show much ingenuity. He describes them as others before him have done, borrowing vocabulary from architecture (domes, igloos, arches) or from the gourmet (apples, peaches, etc.)

The Song of Solomon compared the breasts to 'two young roes that are twins'. We Indians are familiar with comparisons of bosoms with melons and mangoes. We also have allusions to their restlessness: a popular Punjabi folk song sings of them as jangli kabootar—wild pigeons. They have been endowed with an autonomous existence of their own; an otherwise shy, docile damsel may be possessed, as an eighteenth-century English poet wrote, of 'a rugged bosom that beauty cannot tame'.

The male preference for a well-stacked bosomy female is prehistoric. Figurines of goddesses with three breasts predate the Indus Valley civilization. Even later when women shed the third breast, the sizes of the two that remained were of vital interest to the male. A woman who was poorly endowed was always regarded a liability. In the Old Testament brothers lamented 'we have a little sister and she hath no breasts'. Charles Dickens's approach was that of an exhausted old man—for him the ideal breasts were those on which a man could repose, like a pillow. For the more youthful the preference would be for the more shapely, 'on which a man could hang jewels'.

I can understand bosoms being likened to domes or fowl or fruit which they resemble but find it less comprehensible when they are described as edibles. A child may have good reason to call them 'honey pots' but it sounds odd when old Spenser addresses his lady love's adornments as if he were saying grace before supper:

> Was it a dream, or did I see plain?
> A goodly table of pure ivory,
> All spread with junkets, fit to entertain
> The greatest prince with pompous royalty:
> 'Mongst which, there in a silver dish did lie
> Two golden apples of unvalued price...

In another of the *Amoretti* the praise is largely floral:

> Her goodly bosom, like a strawberry bed;
> Her neck, like a bunch of Columbines

Her breast, like lilies, ere their leaves be shed;
Her nipples like young blossomed jessamines.

On erotica my personal preference is for the bawdier form of literature like the limerick. To wit:

To his bride said the keen-eyed detective,
'Can it be that my eyesight's defective?
Has the east tit the least bit
The best of the west tit
Or is it the faulty perspective?'

(1979)

NICK TO THE NAME

There is a bawdy story about a man who lost all his children soon after they were born. He consulted a learned pandit who advised him that he should give his children to come ugly names so that God (who presumably doesn't mouth obscenities) would not send for them. Following the wise man's advice the man named his next son after the male genitals, the daughter who followed after the female genitalia, and being a whole-hogger, named the kid his goat had delivered 'Buttocks'. It worked. The three attained puberty in good health. It is not recorded how the two humans with these peculiar names fared in social circles. But the story reaches its bawdy climax at the nuptials of the girl and her mother's pleading with her son-in-law to be considerate towards her child (named you know what). The irate, un-understanding son-in-law stomps out of the house, and his father-in-law runs after him pleading that he was as dear to him as his own son (you know who?) and if he came back he would slaughter (the Hindi word is maro) the goat-kid to feast him.

There is a moral behind this bawdy tale: only he or she who has to live with it should have the right to choose their name. Since a child has to be called something, the parents may give it a temporary label which its incumbent should be entitled to shed as it sheds its milk teeth and choose another which it fancies.

A much bigger problem is posed by nicknames. These are given unasked and are more often than not meant to hurt. Imagine the agony of an obese child being called Bessie or Billy Bunter, Fatso or Motu! Or of a thin child being called Skinny!

A long-nosed one being a Concorde! A thick-lipped being called Lipso. Often nicknames do not allude to physical features but are mutilations of the real name. For some reason I was nicknamed Shali, which I did not mind too much. But when it came to be rhymed: Shali shooli bagh ki mooli (radish in the garden) I minded it very much. For some mysterious reason Shali died out. I was re-nicknamed

Khusrau which I did not mind too much. But when Khusrau had its tail docked and I was labelled Khusra (eunuch) I minded it very much. Now I read of a poor Indian girl in England with a nice name like Suneeta who has been nicknamed Snot-eater. The vicissitudes through which nicknames pass are infinite. A new publication *Nicknames: Their Origin & Social Consequences* mentions a child nicknamed Polly (Scots for Chubby) successively being re-nicknamed Pearshape, Persia, Iran, Irene, Irebus and, finally, Bus. How right was Hazlitt in his opinion that a nickname is the hardest stone that the Devil can throw at a man!

Seldom do nicknames pursue their bearers into adult life. Then we design all kinds of euphemisms to cover up unpleasant truths. A blind man is a Nainsukh, Surdas, Soorma, or Lakhnetra (with 100,000 eyes). Plutarch mentions that this was a common practice in ancient Athens where a harlot was described as a companion, tax as a donation, a dungeon as a chamber.

Another right that should be granted to all mankind is to change their names to suit a country they happen to be in. I recall an embarrassing encounter with a distinguished Swede, a Mr Lund (very common name in Scandinavia) who was due to visit India. After a few drinks I got the courage to tell him that he should not be upset if northern Indians smiled or sniggered at being introduced to him and explained what his name meant in Hindustani. He was most amused and told me that he had not long before escorted an Indian lady called Miss Das and had to introduce her to various audiences. 'Why should that have embarrassed you?' I asked him. 'Because in Swedish the word "dass" means shit,' replied Mr Lund.

(1979)

O MISTRESS MINE! WHERE ARE YOU ROAMING?

Much ink has been spilt trying to define a mistress; she has proved to be slippier than the proverbial eel. As a matter of fact it is easier to say who is not a mistress than to say with any degree of certainty who is: the classical approach neti neti is best. The point on which all lexicographers are agreed is that a wife is not, nor can ever be the mistress of her own husband. She may be the mistress of his household, boss over his business, even rule over his heart, but if it is a mistress she wants to be, it has to be to a man other than her husband. She must be his 'exclusive keep' and wield influence over him.

Cleveland Amory in *Who Killed Society*? has this dialogue: 'Do you mean to say that the Union Club has come to a day when a man can bring his mistress to a club?' asked an irate member. The doorman knowing the great club tradition replied, 'Sir, you may if the lady is the wife of any of the members.' All dictionaries confirm the common usage of the word that a mistress is 'a woman illicitly occupying the place of a wife'. One of *Playboy* magazine's deft definitions sums it up: 'The difference between a wife and a mistress is night and day.'

Having eliminated the wife, we now proceed to examine the status of other women in their relationships to men. At the bottom of the list is the streetwalker. Seth Sonamal Hirachand Motiwala, having done an honest day's work in his shop, is on his way home in the twilight hour. He is propositioned by a pimp (bharooah) or accosted directly by an overdressed lady. He takes a quick look around, assures himself that he is not recognized by anyone, makes a deal and goes to some dingy room and has what is described in Yankee slang as a 'wham, bam, thank you, ma'am'. He adjusts his dhoti, resumes his customary expression of sanctimonious righteousness and rejoins his happy family. Can the lady recipient of his money and his seed describe herself as his mistress? Certainly not. A 'quickie' does not elevate a woman to the status of a mistress. Even if Seth Sonamal Hirachand Motiwala's constitution only allows him 'quickies', there must be a succession of them stretched over a period of time before the lady in question can claim to have crossed the first hurdle.

What applies to the streetwalkers applies equally to the whore with premises of her own and the call girl at the beck and call of any patron. Seth Sonamal may find it safer and more convenient to do honours to the same lady, but before the lady so patronized can lay claim to the title of Motiwala's mistress, she must fulfil a second qualification–she must acquire a certain measure of influence over Sethji's mind as well as his body. Implicit in this second qualification is the social standing of the paramour. He must be a man of substance and status in society. Poor, nondescript Ghatiamals can, and indeed, do have affairs over prolonged periods of time and their women may acquire stronger holds over them than their wives, but since Ghatiamals have little impact on society, they are not worth reckoning—nor as a consequence are their lady friends. It is only after she has found a man who is rich or powerful, a millionaire, politician or statesman that a woman can call herself a true mistress and throw her weight around.

A third essential qualification is that once the woman takes up with a man she must reserve her favours exclusively for him—or at least appear to be doing so. Thus courtesans, dancing girls and other borderline professionals who serve anyone who pays them are no better than comfort girls attached to the Japanese regiments; they cannot be counted as mistresses. In Indian parlance she must be the exclusive 'keep' of her man.

Having stated the three—or is it four—essentials that go into the making of a mistress, let us now examine some well-known affairs of the mighty of our times. President Roosevelt took a fancy to a society lady and summoned her to the White House. There, without any ceremony, he conducted her to his bedroom, ordered her to strip and leapt on her from his wheelchair (he was a cripple). 'One did not say no to the President of the United States,' explained the lady in her memoirs. Mistress? No. Though bedded by the world's most powerful (politically speaking) man, she wielded no influence over him.

The same applies to the succession of women, including the eminently beddable Marilyn Monroe, who slept with President

Kennedy. And the same disqualification to the one-shot affair of President Nixon. Likewise Lloyd George. Though he sired many bastards, he is not known to have been influenced by their mothers. President Giscard d'Estaing, following the time-honoured tradition of heads of state of France, is reported to have had a liaison with a lady, but it is not known whether or not she in any way guided him and through him the destinies of her great nation.

The institution of the mistress is a universal phenomenon. As one would expect, she is more in evidence in Christian societies where she provides the escape valve to an imposed monogamy than in the Orient where the harem and recognized concubinage provided many an assortment of sexual spice. In India, where love was never regarded as a prerequisite of marriage, it was rare to find men of consequence who did not have mistresses. There is much truth in the statement that where there is marriage without love, there has to be love without marriage.

Our ancient Hindu, Buddhist and Jain aristocracy which looked upon marriage as a kind of treaty between families—to end hostilities, to acquire additional estate or prestige—also sanctioned the keeping of concubines and patronage of courtesans. Some of these ladies became exclusive 'keeps' of their patrons and influenced their decisions.

Pali and Sanskrit have innumerable references to them. In a Sanskrit novel, written in the seventh century CE, a mother describes how she had brought up her daughter, controlling her diet, teaching her astronomy to make her a suitable companion to the potentates of society. But the girl disgraced her calling by falling in love with a young Brahmin who had neither money nor power.

Our epics concede an important status to the veshya. On the eve of the battle of Kurukshetra Yudhishtra is believed to have sent a message of good wishes to the ladies of pleasure: 'My dear friend, ask after the welfare of the fair-decked, fair-clad, scented, pleasure-loving, pleasure-fraught women of the houses of joy.' But these ladies were apparently common whores and could no more claim the status of mistresses than the women who accompanied the army equipped by King Dasharatha for Rama. The Mahabharata also has harsh words for the veshya. On the other hand, the famous Ambapali who entertained the Buddha, though she charged a sizeable fortune for a night, does qualify for the rank of a mistress because the Blessed One conceded: 'This woman moves in worldly circles and is the favourite of kings and princes,' and undoubtedly influenced their judgements.

Muslim conquest and the imposition of Muslim mores drove the Hindu courtesan out of her refined boudoir into the common brothel. Thereafter, the harem became a status symbol—the better stocked, the higher the prestige of the stocker. Any woman that took the fancy of the prince was added to the seraglio as a begum or a rani or, failing that, a concubine. It needed a lot of wiles for one so readily available to gain ascendency as a mistress. Some, however, managed to do so. There was the profligate Jahandar Shah who was so enamoured of a grocer's daughter that he raised many of her relatives to positions of power and even exposed himself naked in a baoli with his mistress in the belief that she would thereby become pregnant. Maharaja Ranjit Singh was said to be greatly influenced by his Muslim 'wife', Bibi Mohran, and had coins struck with her emblem. None of his other wives had much influence over him and it was common knowledge that some of his many Sikh ranis, including Maharani Jindan acclaimed by latter-day Punjabi historians, cuckolded him. The Maharaja had seven strapping sons of whom only the firstborn, Kharak Singh, was accepted as legitimate.

With the coming of the British and their propaganda in favour of monogamy, the mistresses really came into their own. While the wife was put on the shelf of respectability and the common whore reduced to a purely functional role as a gratifier of sexual desire, the mistress became both a companion and a bedmate. She continues to retain her status after Independence. Many of our top-notch statesmen of the establishment and the opposition, topi wallahs, industrialists, ambassadors, senior civil servants and executives are known to keep mistresses. Most of them are provided with jobs, accommodation and other perks such as air-conditioned travel and five-star hotels at government or company expense.

Although it is permissible, indeed in some circles obligatory, to malign mistresses behind their backs, the worldly wise who are in the vast majority will curry favour with them, entertain them in their homes, load them with presents and compliments—none of which they will do for the wives of the people concerned.

Men can be very bitchy about their mistresses. The classic in masculine bitchiness is the repartee between Gladstone and Disraeli—prime ministers of England in succession. Gladstone lashed out: 'Mr Disraeli, you will probably die by the hangman's noose or a vile disease.' The nimble-witted Jew retorted: 'Sir, that depends upon whether I embrace your principles or your mistress.'

The problem with a mistress is the same as with the wife. They both age, become stale and less appealing. Power being the ultimate aphrodisiac (Kissinger), men will retain their potency till deprivation of power castrates them of desire. While on the pedestal they continue to look for new pastures. 'Next to the pleasure of taking a new mistress is that of being rid of an old one,' wrote William Wycherley in *The Country Wife*. The old mistress has to be provided for, or married off to an indigent relative or retainer. If she is literate, she may make some money writing her memoirs. A man with foresight and desire for posthumous respectability can provide against this hazard by inserting a clause in his last will and testament to the effect that if his mistress writes anything about him, the money bequeathed to her should be passed to the wife. Despite all the fun she has, nothing riles a mistress more than the wife.

It would give Shakespeare considerable solace to discover that he would not have to go very far to find his mistress today. She is roaming everywhere, in every country and every city of our civilized world.

(1976)

'By all means!' says the Khosla Commission. 'What you do in private you can project on the screen provided you make the performance a work of art.' Many kissophiles have lined up behind Khosla. I. S. Johar leads the camp with a film devoted entirely to the history and development of the art of kissing from the Vedic period (everything in Hindu India begins with the Vedas) down to the present times. All power to Johar's lips! The kissophobes (i.e. those against public demonstration thereof) appear to be in the majority. 'It is against Hindu tradition,' they say, notwithstanding eloquent testimony to the contrary at Konark, Khajuraho and innumerable other temples and caves. They echo Jonathan Swift's sentiments: 'Lord! I wonder what fool it was that first invented kissing.' But having been invented, there is little excuse to propagate it from the screen, they say. There is substance in this argument. Our film stars are anyhow given to hamming and overacting. If you grant them the liberty to kiss instead of gently rubbing noses or softly joining lips—'a rose-red dot upon the letter i in loving' (Edmond Rostand)—our screen kiss may recall Shakespeare's lines in *The Taming of the Shrew*.

> This done, he took the bride about the neck
> And kiss'd her lips with such a clamorous smack
> That at the parting, all the church did echo

Those who know the reaction of Indian audiences will agree that our cinema halls will not only echo to the 'clamorous smack' of parting lips but also to prolonged derisive smacks, catcalls and whistles. Each kiss on the screen will have to be followed by a ten-minute interval.

There are other hazards. What if the hero or heroine suffers from halitosis or has liberally partaken of garlic or onion before the shooting? The scripted dialogue 'I love you' (how limited we are in expressions of affection!) may suddenly change into a monosyllabic 'ugh'! This may open new vistas to advertisers of breath fresheners and toothpastes—and perhaps the medical profession. Kissing, we are told, can be a serious health hazard as it transfers billions of death-dealing microbes from one amorous mouth to another. But kissing need not necessarily be labial. Walter Savage Landor recommended a pleasanter alternative. 'It is delightful to kiss the eyelashes of the beloved—is it not? But never so delightful as when fresh tears are on them.' It is obvious that Landor never kissed an Indian starlet with kohl or mascara in her eyes. Otherwise he might have taken a darker view on the subject. Well, if you can't kiss on the nose (halitosis) or lips (health), what are the alternatives? Ears? No. It might produce a giggle, even a shiver down the spine. Elsewhere, it may partake of what that naughty and banned-for-obscenity magazine *Playboy* describes as 'an application for a better position'. Thus, notwithstanding the erotica in our places of worship, we say 'No'.

Let the kissophiles and the kissophobes get together and settle the argument—with a kiss. All said and done 'a kiss is a method, cunningly devised, for the mutual prevention of speech at a time when words are superfluous'. (Don Carlson)

On which side am I? I'll tell you through my favourite anecdote on the subject. A hero of World War I was approached by a young girl and asked: 'Did you kill a German?' The hero replied in the affirmative. 'With which hand did you do it?' demanded the girl. 'With this right hand.' The girl took the hand and kissed it. An officer who was watching the proceedings exploded: 'Heavens, man, why didn't you tell her that you bit him to death?'

(1969)

HOO-HA ON WHORING

I once knew a girl, the daughter of a rich and illustrious father. She had an English nanny and tutors who taught her at home. She never went to school or college, nor therefore came by a piece of paper to certify that she was educated. At sixteen she was married to a young man in one of the imperial services. By the time she was twenty-two, she was the mother of three children. She was as happy as she could be because she aspired for nothing more than a husband, children and a home.

Then her world came crashing down. Her father's business collapsed and, rather than face the disgrace of bankruptcy, he took his own life. A few months later, her husband was charged with corruption, dismissed from service and ended up in gaol. Thus, within one year, this mother of three children was left fatherless (her mother had been dead many years), husbandless, homeless and paisaless.

She struggled hard. Since she had no degree, she could not get a job. She took on private tuitions and did odd jobs but was unable to pay the rent of her apartment, feed, clothe and educate her children. Men were willing to, and did, befriend her, but no one was eager to take on a mother of three children on a permanent basis. With some bitterness she said, 'They would take me out, spend lavishly on me, give me expensive presents which were of no use to me. But as soon as I suggested that instead of flowers, saris and ornaments they give me money to pay my children's school fees and doctor's bills, their attitude changed. They became discourteous, used me roughly and treated me as a chattel they could pass to their friends. To them I was a common whore. Technically, I suppose I am. So are a hundred thousand other so-called respectable women: spinsters, married, widowed, divorced, whose chief asset in the eyes of their lovers, husbands and benefactors is their body.'

I relate this true story to illustrate how thin the borderline is between what is acceptable or condoned by society and what is condemned as prostitution. As George Bernard Shaw remarked in *Mrs Warren's Profession*: The only way for a woman to provide for herself decently is for her to be good to some man that can afford to be good to her.'

This brings me to the deliberations of the 25th Abolitionist Conference which was so exercised over the prevalence of prostitution. I was surprised to note that so many delegates, chiefly our own countrymen, continued to adopt the same sanctimonious tone towards their 'fallen sisters' as did their grandparents. And so few had any acquaintance with the research and experience of prostitution in other countries. The problem is vastly exaggerated. In countries like ours it should not be given high priority because there are innumerable others like food, housing, education and employment that must take precedence. We should not encourage our law-enforcing agencies to dissipate their energies raiding brothels and arresting women soliciting in the streets when they are as yet unable to cope with violence, arson, burglary, theft, cheating, adulteration of food, black marketing, etc.

The Conference agreed that prostitution cannot be abolished by simply passing laws. The delegates did not have the courage to go further and say that, in countries where the sexes continue to be segregated as strictly as they are in India, prostitution provides the safety valve for frustrated youth. If the ban were ever to be enforced effectively, crimes of sex would multiply—so would the incidence of violence to person and property. And where did our Attorney General, Mr Niren De, acquire the notion that it is only poverty that drives women to prostitution? He would do well to read *The Psychology of a Prostitute* and Polly Adler's *A House is Not a Home* and learn that innumerable women actually prefer living by prostitution to the drudgery of domestic life or working in offices.

The experience of post-war France should convince everyone of the danger of outlawing prostitution. As soon as licensed brothels were closed, their inmates took to the streets. In brothels they were subjected to regular medical examinations; on their own, they neglected doing so. Venereal disease went up by astronomical proportions. As Harry Golden wrote in *For 2 ¢ Plain*: 'The puritan strain in our culture hounded the professional out of the brothel and forced her to move into the apartment next door, where she quickly became the best tenant.' I suspect that many people who wax eloquent against prostitutes do so because it gives them the opportunity to indulge in talk about sex and yet not mar their holier-than-thou image. If they really mean to abolish prostitution, let them lend an ear to the advice of Alva Myrdal, one-time Swedish ambassador to India. When asked by the dowagers of the All India Women's Conference how the Scandinavian countries had got the better of this problem, she replied with a straight face: 'Ladies, the only way to abolish prostitution is for the amateur to drive out the professional.'

Permissive sex does not breed prostitution, it reduces its incidence.

(1972)

THE KAMASUTRA GAME

Did Vatsyayana know what he was talking about when he classified women into four distinct, easily identifiable categories? Does the modern woman explode his thesis?

Sage Vatsyayana, author of *Kamasutra,* the Hindu treatise on love, classified women into four categories according to their physical characteristics and desires and emotional responses. He placed them in the following order of merit. Padmini, Chitrini, Shankhini and Hastini. The classification can be better comprehended if we reverse the order and start at the bottom.

The Hastini, named after the elephant, is pachydermatous in her proportions: massive, with a large, pumpkin-like bosom, enormous hips and buttocks, expansive thighs and hirsute around private aspects of her anatomy. She has a gargantuan appetite for food, strong liquor and sex. Her body exudes an odour reminiscent of a mahout's wife—if you have been lucky enough to have known one. In the crisis of her excitement she is said to trumpet like a mast (rogue) elephant.

The Shankhini partakes of the nature of the conch shell, she is hard, hollow and sexually as agitated as the Bay of Bengal during a typhoon. In the frenzy of excitement she is known to dig her nails into the flesh of her paramour and scream obscenities like a harlot.

The Chitrini is the arty type: somewhat smaller of bosom and behind than her more amply endowed sisters of the two categories mentioned above. Her appetite for food and sex is correspondingly smaller. She loves music and painting. She likes to put jasmine chaplets in her hair, wear jewellery and fine clothes. She gets more enjoyment from being embraced and kissed than the act of sex.

The fourth category partakes of the lotus flower and is therefore named after it as Padmini. She is petite, demure, with a water lily blush on her damask cheeks. Her eyes are like those of a gazelle and she is therefore also described as mrignayani. And like some species of gazelles, she carries an invisible pod of musk in her navel which envelops anyone fortunate enough to envelop her in his arms. Padmini has a small appetite, she imbibes nothing stronger than cool, clear water—or, perhaps, a lemonade with lots of ice. As the sun sets she folds up her petals as if they were veils and retires to bed. She never uses coarse language, expresses no desire for sex. When taken, she submits with grace as expected of a good Hindu woman. She makes no sounds that may be interpreted as pleasurable. A sigh may escape her lips and with the sigh some expression of thanksgiving to her Creator—Hai Ram!

Vatsyayana, like other great Hindu savants, was prone to reducing every subject on which he wrote into precise categories. He enumerated the varieties of kissing, ways of biting, scratching and sexual pastimes. Modern Hindu scholars have enriched Vatsyayana's enumeration by adding techniques known to the Arabs and the people of France. They are of the considered opinion that not only was Vatsyayana wrong in classifying women into four distinct categories but that he also erred in ascribing specific characteristics to them. There are, for instance, Hastinis who eat very little, are strict teetotallers and abhor sex like the plague. And there are Padminis who guzzle steak carved from the flanks of the holy cow and wash it down with the fiery brew called Asha—desire. The modern generation of students of the Hindu art of love dismiss Vatsyayana as a lot of bull. The following incidents prove how wrong the *Kamasutra* can be as a guide.

Woman-spotting has long been my favourite sport. Bombay is a great city to practise it in. And in Bombay the foyer of the Taj Mahal or the Oberoi-Sheraton is the best place from which to tee off as on a lush eighteen-hole golf course.

According to the rules, foreigners are excluded from the game. Their women are larger than ours and I am not as familiar as I would like to be with their culinary tastes and bed behaviour.

I take my place on the settee facing the reception desk and watch people as they come to register or make enquiries. They present their posteriors for scrutiny. Although the sari is designed to make calculations go awry, with a little practice you can strip off the unnecessary millimetres of colourful camouflage and plant a mental label on their bare behinds. First, comes a large, twin-pumpkin rotunda draped in shimmering chiffon with a dahlia embroidered in the centre in gold. She is chewing paan and surveys the men in the hall to see who will make a nice betel leaf. A Hastini without any doubt. But one must not jump to conclusions without examining the rest of her facade with X-ray eyes. That dahlia covering the rear cleft is somewhat distracting and instead of consulting the *Kamasutra*, I recall the limerick of the young man of Australia, who painted his behind with a dahlia, etc., etc. She strides away behind the porter carrying her valise. No label.

The next one at the reception counter is in a saffron lungi. She is very small with a behind like that of a schoolboy. The clerk at the desk towers above her. She has to stand on her dainty little toes to fill in her name in the register. She turns round. Very petite! Little red dot on her forehead. A smear of sindoor in the parting of her hair to indicate her marital status and a black-beaded mangalsutra to reinforce it. Where is her husband? She gives the porter a rupee note and tells him to take her bag to her room and leave the keys at the reception. She catches me ogling at her. A faint lily blush comes over her face. Padmini. A hundred-paise worth of Padmini in the rupee.

My 100 per cent Padmini glides down the corridor. She reminds me of Robert Herrick's lines:

> When as in silks my Julia goes,
> methinks how gently flows the
> liquefaction of her lungi.

She casts a sidelong glance at a boutique window, abruptly turns right and disappears from view. 'Not the Harbour Bar?' I almost scream to myself. What would a Padmini be doing amongst the dissolute lot who foregather in that dim, vice-laden madhushala? She must have gone up to the Rendezvous to join her husband, or brother, or father. I saunter down to the elevators and take one to the rooftop restaurant. I brush aside the steward and scan the faces of the diners. No Padminis there. Three or four likely Chitrinis and one Hastini.

I take the elevator down to the reception and saunter into the Harbour Bar. There she is! Demurely perched on a tall stool, fixing a cigarette in a long ebony cigarette holder. I take the stool alongside with an air of bored indifference. The barman lights her cigarette. She rummages inside her handbag, finds her health permit and slaps it on the bar. 'Scotch on the rocks, make it a double.' She pouts her lips and sends rings of blue smoke like the emblems of the Olympic games floating into the room. Two more jets shoot downwards from her nostrils, recoil on her lungi and then settle back in her saffron lap. While the barman is pouring out a large Scotch for her, she stretches her arm, draws a bowlful of pickled onions towards her and tosses three into her dainty mouth. This is tamasik (stale) food, wholly unsuitable diet for a Padmini.

The barman gives me a glass of lager. I steal a pearl onion from her bowl. She ignores my presence. In two gulps Padmini disposes of the Scotch and onion bowl. The barman pours in another double into her glass. She looks questioningly at him. He explains, 'That gentleman over there in the corner! With his compliments.'

Padmini turns her gazelle eyes towards the corner. The gentleman flashes a gold-studded denture and waves a hand laden with sparklers. Padmini ignores him. Without as much as a smile of thanks she returns to her Scotch on the rocks. The second large Scotch goes down the lovely hatch; a second bowl of raw onions is emptied. When the barman pours the third burra Scotch, Padmini merely asks, 'The same chap, no? Who is he?'

'Yes, madam,' replies the barman in a tone heavy with reverence. 'He, richest, richest man of Bombay.' I don't catch his name, but it sounds something like 'Seth Hiralal Sonamal Magnolia'. Padmini is unimpressed. She simply drains the Scotch and holds out the tumbler to the barman. 'Can I have another large one? Put it on the fat bastard's bill.'

My faith in Vatsyayana's classification is rudely shaken. The image of the chastity and incorruptibility of Hindu womanhood is on the verge of being shattered. Surely any woman who accepts drinks from a total stranger can have little compunction in expressing her gratitude in the conventional way! But, as I said before, don't jump to conclusions. Padmini has had her regular quota of four large whiskies and two bowls of raw onions. She asks for her health permit and the bill for the first drink. 'Taken care of, madam,' replies the barman. Padmini puts her cigarette holder in her bag and slides off the stool. Seth Hiralal Sonamal Magnolia threads his way through tables of drinkers and comes to stake his claim. 'Good evening, madam!' he says, with an ingratiating smile. 'Would you care to join me for dinner? I am Seth Hiralal Sonamal Magnolia.'

The moment of truth has arrived. If she says yes, it would be clear proof that though she looks like a virgin Padmini, she is in fact a Hastini slut. If she politely rebuffs the richest man of Bombay she redeems her status as a Padmini.

Padmini gives Seth Magnolia an icy stare. And in words loud enough to be heard by everyone in the Harbour Bar hisses, 'Seth Hiralal Sonamal, you know what? I'd like to be your widow. Now buzz off!'

(1974)

ME, THE JOKERMAN

OVERHEARD IN PAKISTAN

President General Zia-ul-Haq desired to issue a postage stamp to commemorate his two-year rule in Pakistan. The best artist of the country was ordered to draw his portrait: Sam Browne belt, medals, epaulettes, the works. Millions of stamps were printed and released with great fanfare. After a couple of weeks the President wanted to know how the stamp was doing. He sent for the Post Master General and asked him about the sales.

'General President, sir, I deeply regret to inform you that the stamp is not selling well.'

'Why?'

'Because they do not stick.'

'Why? Have the gum supplier arrested immediately. I will have him flogged publicly.'

'No sir, there is nothing wrong with the gum,' protested the Post Master General, 'the stamps won't stick because the people put their spit on the wrong side.'

(1980)

NOT HEARD IN PAKISTAN

General Zia-ul-Haq while on a visit to India decides to ring up the late Mr Bhutto to find out how he is getting on wherever he is. He puts in a long distance call. Indian telephones, which have great difficulty in putting through local calls, have no trouble whatsoever connecting him with the nether regions. So General Zia has a brief three-minute chat with Bhutto who assures him he is better looked after than he was in Rawalpindi gaol. General Zia's telephone bill for this long distance call is Rs 1000. This is understandable as hell is a long way away from India.

General Zia returns to Pakistan and decides to have another pow-wow with the late Mr Bhutto. Pakistan telephones have learnt the ropes from their Indian counterparts and immediately get Mr Bhutto on the line. General Zia talks to Bhutto for over an hour. He then asks for the bill. It is only Rs 15. The General is most impressed but asks his telephone department to explain how a three-minute call from India cost him a thousand rupees while an hour's chat from Pakistan cost only fifteen. Promptly comes the reply: 'Sir, in Pakistan a call to hell is charged at local rates.'

(1979)

I did not find any special Pakistani flavour in the jokes about their leaders. One often related about General Ayub Khan I had heard about Indira Gandhi. The General arrives in Allah's court where there is a large assemblage of the world's great personages. The Almighty honours them by getting up from his throne to shake hands with them. But when General Ayub Khan steps forward to greet his Maker, Allah remains firmly seated on his throne. Later, the angels gather round Allah and ask him about his strange behaviour in discriminating against the distinguished Pakistani. Allah replies: 'With the others I felt quite safe, but I know that if I left my throne to shake hands with Ayub Khan he would immediately push me away and grab it.'

◆

One which I had not heard before applies equally to the Indian situation as it does to the Pakistani. There has been a prolonged drought, an entire crop ruined because of the failure of the monsoon. A delegation of Pakistani ulema approach Allah and beg for rain. The Almighty replies: 'We have run out of clouds. If you don't believe us you can inspect all our godowns.' The pious ulema, though not distrustful of Allah, nevertheless undertake a tour of inspection. Godown after godown but not a cloud in them. Then suddenly they come upon a black, rain-bearing nimbus cloud. They return to Allah and inform him of their discovery. Allah replies: 'Oh, that one; that is reserved to cause floods in your country.'

◆

General Zia comes in for the usual brand of humour that builds around heads of state. It is well known that his dour image as a stern disciplinarian conceals a man unsure of himself and prone to change his opinion. Hence his designation as Chief Marshal Law Administrator (CMLA) is often rendered as Change My Last Announcement. The

Nizam-i-Mustafa has generated a crop of jokes largely around hand chopping (no one has yet been deprived of his limb) and the drinking behind drawn curtains. There is the story of a well-known bowler found guilty of having stolen goods from a store. His lawyer, pleading for a lighter sentence, appeals to the judge: 'While passing sentence, your honour may take into account that the accused person is the best left-arm spin bowler of Pakistan.'

◆

Drinking has been drastically cut down. But it is well known that in multi-storeyed hotels served by lifts the management put their elevators out of commission after dark. The police seldom have the enthusiasm to climb up fourteen or more floors. So liquor flows with the abandon of the Indus. The top floors of hotels are described as the last bastions of resistance against the Nizam-i-Mustafa.

(1979)

HOT TALES FROM PAKISTAN

Recent visitors to our militant neighbour have brought back a crop of anecdotes bearing on its state of affairs. The first one compares it to its neighbour on the other side, Iran.

Ayatollah Khomeini called on Allah and complained: 'Just and merciful Allah! I have introduced the Islamic code in my country but there has been no improvement in the condition of the people. When will things change for the better?'

Allah thought over the problem for a minute and replied, 'Not in your lifetime.'

Khomeini burst into tears and departed.

The next caller was General Zia-ul-Haq. 'Almighty God, I have also introduced the Islamic code in my country and there has been no improvement in the condition of the people. When will things get better in Pakistan?'

Allah pondered over the problem for a minute and burst into tears and replied, 'Not in my lifetime.'

◆

A peasant travelling by bus from Rawalpindi to Islamabad addressed the man sitting next to him, 'Sir, are you in the army?'

'No.'

'Is your brother or any other relation in the army?'

'No.'

'Is there anyone from your village in the army?'

'No.'

'In that case, you son-of-a-bitch, why the hell have you put your foot on mine?'

◆

Three civilians were hauled up before a military court for assaulting an army captain. When asked to explain, the first accused replied,

'Sir, this man winked at my sister and I felt I had to beat him up to redeem her honour.'

The second accused replied: 'Sir, every girl in the village is like a sister to me. So when this fellow winked at my friend's sister I joined him in redeeming the girl's honour.'

The third accused who was not from the village replied: 'Sir, when I saw these two men assault the man in uniform, I thought that military rule was over in Pakistan, so I said to myself, why not I also do something for my country?'

(1980)

'TAIL' PIECE

It is a great pity our legislators lose their tempers so readily. Much more can be achieved by ready wit than by angry demonstrations, yelling slogans, abuse, fisticuffs or walkouts. I recall an encounter between the late Feroze Gandhi and a senior cabinet minister given to making acid remarks about everyone and with an exaggerated notion of his own ability. This minister was said to have described Feroze Gandhi as the 'Prime Minister's lapdog'. Then he had the misfortune of getting involved in a financial scandal. Feroze Gandhi was scheduled to open the debate in the Lok Sabha. He is said to have walked up to the minister and within the hearing of the Treasury benches said: 'Mr So-and-so, I hear you have been describing me as a lapdog. You no doubt consider yourself a pillar of the state. Today I will do to you what a dog usually does to a pillar.'

(1969)

BABU EXPLOSION

Two tigers who had escaped from the Delhi Zoo reappeared in their respective cages after six months of freedom. One was very fat, the other reduced to skin and bone. They began to discuss their experiences. Said the thin one: 'I was very unlucky. I found my way to Rajasthan. There was famine. I could not get enough to eat. Even the cattle I killed had no flesh on them. I would have died of hunger, so I decided to surrender myself to the police. Although I am caged here, at least I get my bellyful of meat every day.'

He asked his fat companion why he had come back to the zoo. 'At first I had very good luck,' replied the fat tiger, licking his chops in happy reminiscence. 'I got into the secretariat buildings and hid myself under a staircase. Every evening, as the millions of babus poured out of their offices, I used to catch one and eat him up. For the first six months no one noticed anything. But yesterday I made the mistake of eating up the fellow who serves them their relays of cups of tea and coffee. Then they let hell loose on me. Take my word, it is safer behind bars than being at the mercy of those bloodthirsty babus.'

◆

You've probably heard this one before. Maybe you have your own favourite story to illustrate the explosive birth rate in our bureaucracy. If you wish to see concrete proof, take Delhi's telephone directory of 1929 and that of 1969 and compare the number of officials in each. Thirty years ago a handful of civil servants with a few underlings administered this country, including areas which are now Pakistan. Today a smaller area requires almost four times as many officials to look after it. Count the number of secretaries of various hues—secretary general, special secretaries, additional secretaries, joint secretaries, deputy secretaries and undersecretaries—add the number of officers on special duty, the hordes of superintendents, section officers, clerks, stenographers, typists and peons. The figure runs into the thousands, their salaries into astronomical figures. What is incredible is that we know that more hands mean more red tape and less efficiency. But we seem to be unable to check the proliferation of government departments and civil servants. What Robert Malthus said about population increasing in geometrical progression, Cyril Northcote Parkinson said about bureaucracy. But whereas the Malthusian multiplication can be curbed by the pill and the loop, no one has yet devised anything to prevent the fecund bureaucrat from generating larger and larger litters of babus, big and small.

(1969)

USHA-LOVES-RAKESH-USHA

I am an ardent collector of graffiti—scribbling on walls. In the West this art is usually practised in public lavatories. In India one seldom sees anything besides names and dates defacing historic monuments or the attaching of whiskers, beards or pudenda to pictures of women on hoardings. It is different in the hills where the climate is somewhat Western. Himachal has many rain shelters. Visitors trapped by the monsoon find the white walls of shelters and the easy supply of burnt wood left by departed picnickers very tempting. One such shelter at Kasauli is like the town's wall newspaper. From its graffiti I learn who loves who, of the lustiest maiden in town—frequently illustrated by line drawings of the wench in action. Most of the writing is in Hindi verse. But students of Lawrence Public School across the hill at Sanawar make their contributions in English. The walls have to be frequently whitewashed. Last time I went to the Kasauli rain shelter, I saw a notice put up by the Cantonment Board: 'Do not write on the walls'. A few days later a line appeared underneath—I give the credit to a Lawrencian—'Do you want it to be typed?'

(1969)

'GOOD SHOT, SIR...'

Cricket is very much in the air. Most of us are now convinced we are no better at this game than at others. We live on memories of our great masters: Ranji, Duleep, Nayudu, Pataudi, Nissar, Wazir Ali. Those were names to be reckoned with. But I have this true anecdote from a test match between England and Australia at Lord's. Duleepsinhji had gone in to bat for England. An English spectator turned to his Australian neighbour and asked him whether they had any princes in their team. The crestfallen Australian shook his head. 'We have,' said the Englishman very proudly, 'that fellow there is a maharaja—palaces, elephants, harems—and a damn good bat too.' Duleepsinhji obliged by hitting a six. 'Good shot, sir,' bellowed the Englishman. 'See what I mean? One of the greatest batsmen of our time.' On the next ball Duleepsinhji's middle stump flew into the air. The same Englishman screamed, 'He's out. The bloody nigger!'

(1969)

TO DIE, EXPIRE, PERCHANCE TO...

I scan the 'death' columns of most daily papers. 'But for the grace of God', I say to myself, 'I would be seeing my own name in print.' Could any reader enlighten me why Punjabis 'leave for their heavenly abode', Bengalis 'pass on', and all other Indians simply 'expire'?

(1969)

ME, THE JOKERMAN

I have a large collection of jokes: some I make myself, others I pick up from friends or books and remould to suit me. Several slim volumes of my jokes liberally contributed to by readers have been published and sell better than any of my other books. I get the royalties, my contributing readers only get the pleasure of seeing their names in print. The joke is on them. Unfortunately, most of my best jokes are unprintable because they have to do with sex aberrations. What is a joke if it hasn't something to do with sex? Book censors don't see it that way.

My second best jokes are about my own community, the Sardarjis. At one time they had the confidence to laugh at themselves. No longer so. They have become as touchy as Tamil Brahmins who happily laugh at jokes about Marwaris, Chettiars, Bengalis, Parsis and Mian-bhais; but you tell one joke about them and they are up in arms.

I will tell you a few of my favourite jokes that are printable. If you have heard one before, skip it and get on to the next one. The first is one about Sardarjis of the Ramgarhias caste, the same as Giani Zail Singh, whose main profession is carpentry.

Two Sikh carpenters settled in London were reminiscing about their good fortune since they immigrated to England. Said one, 'The Guru has been good to us. In India we were poor carpenters. And, see, here we have our own house, our own car, TV set, Frigidaire, washing machine. We've got everything we could ask for.'

'True,' replied the other, 'we have all we wanted except one thing. We've never had a white woman.'

'That can be easily done,' said the other. 'I'll get one from the streets and ask her to join us.'

So one went out and soon brought a white girl home. The only trouble was that the Sardarji spoke no English and the girl spoke no Punjabi. After a long moment of silence, the girl picked up a plate from the table and with her lipstick drew the picture of a bottle. 'She wants whisky,' said the Sardarji.

So they got a bottle of whisky. After another spell of silence, the girl wiped out the picture of the bottle and drew one of a bird.

'She wants to eat chicken,' deciphered the Sardar.

So they brought a tandoori chicken and the three ate it.

After yet another period of silence, the girl drew a picture of a bed on the plate.

'How in hell did she get to know we were carpenters?' shouted both the Sardarjis.

Saved on the verge of being a dirty joke. This one is somewhat political and also clean. It was told during the time Indira Gandhi imposed Emergency on the country. Bapu Gandhi in heaven was very perturbed that after all he had done for the country no one really bothered about him anymore. So he sent for Nehru, who was also in heaven, and asked him, 'Nehru, what did you do all the years you were prime minister to perpetuate my memory?' Nehru replied, 'Bapu, I did all I could. I had a Samadhi made at the spot where we cremated you. Twice in the year, your birthday and the day of your assassination, we collected in the thousands to sing 'Ram Dhun' and pay homage to you.'

Bapu was satisfied with Nehru's answer. He sent for Lal Bahadur Shastri and put to him the same question, 'Bapu, I had a very short time as prime minister,' replied Shastri. 'In those two and a half years I had all your works and speeches translated into all the Indian languages and put in village libraries.'

Gandhi was satisfied. 'Who became PM after you?' he asked.

'It is Nehru's chhokri who is ruling the country now,' he replied.

So Bapu sent for Indira Gandhi and put the same question to her. Indira replied, 'I've done more to perpetuate your memory than either my father or Shastri. I've made the entire populace like you and left them with nothing more than a loincloth of the type you wear and a stick of the sort you carry.'

Bapu was very alarmed. 'You mustn't do this. The people will rise in rebellion against you,' he warned.

'I've taken care of that,' replied Indira. 'I let them carry the langoti in their hands and have stuck the stick up their bottoms.'

◆

This last one is again a Sardarji joke. But restricted to one, our ex-president Giani Zail Singh. When Indira Gandhi had him elected president she began to doubt the wisdom of her choice. She called a cabinet meeting and told them, 'Giani speaks no English. How will he communicate with other heads of states?'

They pondered over the problem and decided that Gianiji should be given an English tutor. 'But only a head of state should teach the head of our state,' was the cabinet consensus.

So a global tender was floated for a head of state to teach Gianiji English. Only Ronald Reagan applied. 'You send him over to the White House for six months and I'll have him speaking English like a Yank,' he wrote.

So Gianiji was flown to Washington and was a house guest of the Reagans. After six months Indira sent for Rajiv and said, 'Our president has been missing for a long time. You go to Washington, find out how much English he has learnt and bring him back.'

So Rajiv flew to Washington and called on the Reagans at the White House. 'Mr President, I've come to fetch Gianiji and find out how much English you have taught him.'

Reagan replied in rustic Punjabi, 'Iss munday nun angrezee kadee nahin aunee—this lad will never pick up English.'

(Undated)

SARDARJI HAS THE LAST LAUGH

'Have you heard this one about Milkha Singh? Well, there was this Flying Sikh—'

'Are you relaxing? No, I am Milkha Singh.' Heard it half a century ago.

Milkha isn't fifty so you couldn't have heard it half a century ago. In any case, he wasn't relaxing. He was sleeping soundly in his village home when a thief broke in. He happened to drop something. The crash woke up Milkha. The thief ran. Milkha sprinted at Olympic speed after him. On the way he ran into another Sardarji.

'Milkha Singhji, where you heading for at this pace at this hour of the night?'

'Chasing a thief.'

'A thief? Where is he?'

'Oh, I left him far behind.'

Bet you hadn't heard that before! Ha ha ha!

(1972)

MISSISSIPPI IN TAMIL NADU

A young reader sends a south Indian version of how to spell Mississippi. First comes *yumma.* Then *I* come. Then my *sissi.* Then I *p-p*. Then *I* come again.

(1971)

GALBRAITH IS GREAT FUN

John Kenneth Galbraith's *Ambassador's Journal* about his two and a half years as the US ambassador in Delhi has been published. Galbraith is no common man—he is as towering a personality as he is in person—six foot six inches, vain as a giraffe ('Modesty is a vastly overrated virtue,' says he) and with little respect for anyone's intelligence save his own. It is no wonder he did not get on with men as self-opinionated as himself. Galbraith's and Krishna Menon's views about each other would take up quite a few columns in the dictionary of insults. Although he thinks of few men as his mental equals, Galbraith has always been impressed by power. To him Kennedy was like a young god; Nehru had irresistible charisma (in Delhi Galbraith was 'a pandit who walked with Pandits yet kept his uncommon touch'—Gore Vidal); he saw eye to eye with the equally statured De Gaulle 'that the world belongs to the tall men'.

Galbraith is great fun. He is a very gifted raconteur. He once told me of the experiences of an American couple who came with an introduction to 'Mr Singh of Delhi'. Their friends had assured them, 'you cannot miss him. He wears a turban and a beard and drives a cab.' The poor couple had the misfortune of running into a Mr Singh who answered to the description and proceeded to take the Americans for a ride. (The Americans' naiveté has to be experienced to be believed!) Mr Singh presented them with a bill of Rs 400 for two days of sightseeing. By then they had noticed that most of the city's cabs were plied by men with turbans and beards—and almost all of them answered to the name Singh.

Galbraith's favourite after-dinner anecdote was about his visit to Bengal. A very enthusiastic officer from the department of agriculture was appointed to escort him on a tour of the countryside. The young man went on endlessly about plans, projects, hydro-electric power, afforestation, compost pits, etc. In order to show some interest in his surroundings Galbraith pointed to a clump of eucalyptus trees and asked, 'Are they indigenous?'

'Oh yes, sir, they are very indigenous,' replied the agriculture expert. 'We got them from Australia.'

(1969)

HEARD IN PAKISTAN

Yahya Khan, trying to persuade a yokel to volunteer for the Pakistani Air Force, took him inside the aircraft and explained: 'You press this yellow button and the engine will start. Then you press the red one and the plane will fly. It is all very simple.'

'But how do I bring it down?' asked the yokel, puzzled.

'You don't have to bother about that,' explained Yahya Khan. 'Leave that to the Indian Air Force.'

(1971)

HA HA HONORIS CAUSA

The University of Manila has decided to introduce a three-year course of study in humour. This is no laughing matter. Humour is serious business. It can have a curriculum as varied as any: wit, repartee, calculated insults, epigrams, puns, riddles, limericks, clerihews, shaggy dog stories, bawdy jokes, sick jokes, clean jokes, mother-in-law jokes, racial humour and what have you. As soon as other universities begin to award degrees in humour, you will see that no one will thereafter consider humour a subject for laughter.

I hope very much our schools and colleges will introduce humour as a subject of study. I know few people in the world with a poorer sense of humour than us Indians. We take ourselves too seriously. Many foreigners have remarked that Indians seldom smile. We are touchy about many things and are quick to take offence. Consequently, our aggressive instincts remain bottled up inside us till they explode in anger and violence.

First thing to do is clear our minds about what is humorous. The basis of humour is the puncturing of another person's ego, causing him or her some kind of embarrassment which makes him or her lose his or her dignity. All laughter is at some other person's expense. A man slips on a banana skin and even though his buttocks may be seriously bruised, you burst out laughing. A much-respected citizen is unable to contain the wind in his stomach and farts in public. He cannot thereafter face his fellow citizens and his respect is lost forever. You who enjoy farting in private revel in the other fellow's discomfiture, tell everyone about it and laugh and laugh till tears roll down your cheeks. Malice is the essence of jest. Jest is an important safety valve to preserve one's sanity against the pressure of accumulated malice.

Psychologists also believe that laughter is necessary to keep the balance of mind. A hearty laugh releases aggressive impulses because it is always at someone else's expense. You will notice that people who do not laugh are often constipated with hate. Psychologists also tell us that the ability to see the ridiculous develops very early in a human child. Watch a baby gurgle and chortle, become helpless with laughter when its parents make asinine noises or play peekaboo with it. By the age of seven you can detect whether or not your child will develop into a good raconteur. The ability to tell a joke is inborn. One child of seven will know how to tell a story with a straight face, how long a pause to make before delivering the punchline. Another will ruin the same story by beginning to laugh while telling it and, by forgetting the all-essential pause to create a sense of expectancy, deliver the punchline in a hurry and so murder the joke. Training in storytelling may improve the child a little, but not very much. Storytellers, like mathematicians, are born not made.

It stands to reason that humour is as old as humanity itself. Long before we learnt to write we were making fun of each other. As usual, the Greeks were the first people to record different varieties of humour. The earliest recorded joke I have come across is repartee between an elderly Greek woman driving her herd of asses and a cheeky young man.

'Good morning, mother of asses,' greeted the youngster.

'Good morning, my son,' replied the woman.

We Indians have a rich heritage of humour. We have been profligate and frittered away our storehouse of laughter. We have had our Tenali Ramans and Birbals. What are we left with? Bawdy jokes lifted from foreign sources, jokes about different communities (Bohris, Sardarjis, Marwaris, Parsis, etc.) which we dare not repeat in front of the subjects of our humour and which no one dare print for fear of invoking sections of the Penal Code for causing hatred between the communities.

We must cultivate a sense of humour and learn to laugh at ourselves. But have no illusions about the price you will have to pay. Laughter and success do not go together. You have to choose between being a VIP and being a jester. Thomas Corwin, a member of the US Congress, put it very succinctly: 'Never make people laugh. If you would succeed in life you must be solemn, solemn as an ass. All the great monuments are built over solemn asses.'

We Indians may have lost our sense of humour but we still have a rich laboratory of materials to work on. Every third Indian is a clown in his own right: self-esteem, immodesty, sanctimoniousness, name-dropping and verbosity make a golden treasury of the ridiculous. We could study all these aspects, channel them into stories and then grant degrees to the more laugh-producing dissertations. We could make a very spectacular start by awarding doctorates even before the courses in humour are launched by conferring on our politicians degrees of Ha Ha Honoris Causa!

◆

The latest joke from Czechoslovakia is a dialogue between an official assigned to gauge public opinion and a peasant. The official made his questionnaire as simple as possible for the rustic's mind: 'Now, Jan, if you were asked to make three wishes for your country, what would they be?'

'First, I would wish the People's Liberation Army of the People's Republic of Red China to occupy Czechoslovakia.'

The official refused to be put out of countenance. 'And what would be your second wish?'

'My second wish would be that the People's Liberation Army of the People's Republic of Red China should occupy Czechoslovakia.'

'Okay, okay! That's the same wish twice. What would be your third wish?'

'My third wish would be that the People's Liberation Army of the People's Republic of Red China should occupy Czechoslovakia for the third time.'

'Now, aren't you being a little perverse? Why would you wish your country to be invaded and occupied three times by a foreign army?'

'That's very simple,' replied Jan. 'The People's Liberation Army of Red China would first have to march across and occupy the Soviet Union three times before it could get to us. That would teach the Russians what it means to be under foreign occupation.'

(1970)

ENGLISH BHASHA, DOWN, DOWN

A firm which undertakes to destroy vermin has sent me its terms of contract. If its ability to kill pests is as great as its ability to kill the English bhasha then I can strongly commend it. Instructions are:

(1) Before start the work empted every thing.
(2) In the bed Room Cuboards to be empted.
(3) When the Job is started, nobody can stay inside after fumigation to keep two hours in the Flat
(4) After open the Flat only clean with dry cloth.

(1970)

LITERARY NUGGETS

Every mail brings me some gems of Indo-Anglian literature. One of them addresses me as the 'Respective Singhji' and forewarns himself: 'I must not take your more time.' He seeks my forbearance because 'it is my last but one letter to you. Only one request I want to offer you.' The proffered request is to include him in the list of VIPs of the Chandraseniya Kayastha Prabhus, scheduled for the issue of 26 July. And why not? He is a very important lance naik in our army.

Then there is the entirely lovable Mr Bhatt, a banker who can 'converse in verse'. The rhyming pattern is very simple:

There is none to sue
There is none to coo
There is none to woo
O! God. What should do?

I cannot advise Mr Bhatt on what he should do. But when he proceeds to compose a verse on a lady named 'Devyani' and rhymes it with biryani, it is time to call a halt to versification.

There is also the indefatigable Sardar Daljit Singh Narula who sends me reams of poetry on every important event. The last one was on the election of Ceylon's lady prime minister:

The gun, my pen
Fires a salute
To the Hon'ble Lady Number one.
Of the Salvo Ten Mrs Sirimavo Dias Bandaranaike.

But *The Statesman* of Calcutta has an absolute nugget, said to be a complaint addressed to the District Traffic Superintendent:

Beloved Sir—I am arrive by passenger train at Ahmedpore Station and my belly is too much swelling with jack-fruit. I am therefore want to privy. Just as I doing nuisance, that guard making whistle blow for train to go off and I am running with lota in one hand and dhoti in the next, when I fall over and expose some of my personal thing to many female women on the platform. I am get leaved on Ahmedpore Station. This is too much bad. If passenger go to make dung, that dam guard not wait train five minutes for him. I am therefore pray your honour to make big fine on that dam guard for public sake, otherwise I am making big report to papers.

(1970)

ACKNOWLEDGEMENTS

Many of the essays that appear in this volume are versions of pieces that first appeared in *Yojana*, *New Delhi*, *The Tribune*, *The Statesman*, the *Hindustan Times*, *Illustrated Weekly of India*, and *Times of India*, to name a few of the publications that Khushwant Singh contributed to. As the majority of the pieces were taken from typescripts in the possession of the author's estate, it has been difficult to accurately source the name of the publication in which the pieces first appeared. All the essays in the book have been used with permission from the author's estate. Every effort has been made to trace copyright holders and obtain permission to reproduce copyright material included in the book. In the event of any inadvertent omission, the publisher should be informed and formal acknowledgement will be included in all future editions of this book.

www.ingramcontent.com/pod-product-compliance
Lightning Source LLC
Chambersburg PA
CBHW020811300326
41914CB00075B/1680/J
* 9 7 8 9 3 8 4 0 6 7 5 1 9 *